Your Natural Gifts

Your Natural Gifts

*How to recognize
and develop them
for success and self-fulfillment*

Margaret E. Broadley

EPM Publications, Inc.
McLean, Virginia

Library of Congress Cataloging in Publication Data

Broadley, Margaret E.
   Your natural gifts.

    1. Occupational aptitude tests. I. Title:
Human Engineering Laboratory.
HF5381.B76   1977   153.9′4   77-23379
ISBN 0-914440-19-5

About the Author

Margaret E. Broadley, author of two best-selling books on human aptitudes, has helped all kinds of people discover and develop their inborn abilities. In YOUR NATURAL GIFTS, she sums up all that she has learned through her long friendship with the distinguished pioneer in the field of aptitude testing, Johnson O'Connor.

Her zest for inquiry and experimentation showed up early in Mrs. Broadley's career, leading her into an unusual assortment of jobs. Born in Iowa of Swedish immigrant parents, she graduated from Iowa State University and got her first job with the dairy industry in Chicago. Her work consisted primarily of taking a cage of white rats on the road to demonstrate the supposed dietary advantages of butter over oleo. (One rat died.) Next she was sent to Connecticut where she produced plays in schools and gave thousands of magic lantern talks. Back in Chicago she ran a radio program for a biscuit manufacturer and spent time in his factory. She was Chicago's Queen of Health in the Diamond Jubilee parade in 1931.

Marriage to Charles Broadley took her next to Boston where she sold jewelry in a department store. In New York she worked again for the dairy industry, doing advertising and publicity. She also handled publicity for the first Career Women's Dinner, honoring women such as Ethel Barrymore, Fanny Hurst and Dorothy Shaver.

Mrs. Broadley is the mother of two daughters, both artists, and the grandmother of six children. While rearing her daughters, she worked at her home in Washington, D. C. writing pamphlets, books and articles for magazines from *Life* to *Mademoiselle*. After her children were grown, she wrote for the Red Cross, the White House Conference on Education, USIA and the Labor Department from where she retired in 1969, after 42 years of careers.

Retirement has given Mrs. Broadley more time for reading, gardening, music and travel. Because she planned well for her later years, as she advises people to do in YOUR NATURAL GIFTS, she continues to enjoy an active, richly self-fulfilling life.

223415

To Johnson O'Connor, whose inspired genius and life-long devotion to opening new paths to understanding our natural gifts has given help and hope to many thousands, this book is humbly and lovingly dedicated.

Contents

A Personal Note

Most of us have little, if any, idea of what we were born to do best, of how we can truly express ourselves and live lives that give us some kind of inner satisfaction and a feeling of self-fulfillment. Poets and philosophers long have assured us that the secret lies in being true to ourselves—or in today's vernacular, "doing our own thing." But how can we do it if we don't know what our particular "thing" might be?

Man has achieved an incredible understanding of materials, of atomic nuclei, of magnetic fields, of steel structures; he has walked on the moon and is reaching farther and farther into outer space and into the ocean depths. Yet when it comes to understanding his own behavior and that of his neighbor's he is woefully behind. Far too often he is caught up in the world of material things and life slips by, leaving him with a sense of having missed what he really wanted.

The greatest need in the world today is for more understanding of why we behave as we do, of knowing our strong points and our shortcomings, and where in this complex world we can find and be true to ourselves. If we can't understand and get along with ourselves, how can we expect to get along with others? Many of today's most knotty problems have roots in our lack of human understanding and the too often frustrating search for self-fulfillment.

Probably the full answer to the problem of human understanding never can be found, for there are factors in life far beyond the scope of human knowledge. But it is heartening to know that various groups are probing the mystique of human behavior, using a variety of approaches. This book is about one of these groups, the Human Engineering Laboratory-Johnson O'Connor Research Foundation, who have been pioneers in applying the experimental method of the sciences that led to material progress toward the study of people. They started with the concept that it might be possible to isolate inborn human traits, much as chemists isolated the elements, with research based on fact, reason and calculation, rather than on emotion and imagination.

In other words, the Laboratory's work is dedicated to the finding and measurement of inborn traits, to learn how these natural talents typically combine in the various kinds of work in today's world, and how possession of the different aptitudes influences our behavior. So far, nineteen of these inborn traits have been isolated and can be measured by tests with remarkable accuracy; tests for many more traits are in the experimental stage. The information comes from administering carefully devised worksamples to all kinds of people to learn what traits and combinations of these traits seem to characterize the most successful in particular fields. Well over half a million people have taken the tests since the research began more than half a century ago. Extensive follow-up studies of many who took the tests twenty and thirty years ago verify the validity of this knowledge and give concrete hope and help to a great number of persons, even those who are not personally able to take the tests.

My own interest in the Laboratory's work stems from the help my husband and I derived from it personally, an interest that has grown steadily for more than thirty-six years as the truth of the findings have checked out in real life. Over the years, my knowledge has been gained through a long and close association with the staff of test administrators and research persons located throughout the country, and particularly with the founder, Johnson O'Connor, and with his wife Eleanor, a graduate of M.I.T. and a lifetime architect and teacher.

I first met Mr. O'Connor early in 1941 at the Stevens Institute of Technology in Hoboken, New Jersey, where some of the work of the Human Engineering Laboratory was being carried on, and I had come to take the tests. At the time, we were living outside of New York and my husband commuted to his job in the city. I had left my work in advertising and publicity to stay home and care for our two little daughters, then aged about one and three. The only flaw in an otherwise wonderful life was that my husband was unhappy in his work and could not understand why. A graduate of the Naval Academy, he had left the Navy after two years and gone into private business, working in various aspects of engineering because that was what his training had been.

It was an article by Johnson O'Connor in the *Atlantic Monthly* that had acquainted us with the Human Engineering Laboratory. My husband found it so intriguing he decided he would take the tests at Stevens Institute to see if they might help to clarify his problem.

His taking the tests was a revelation and a turning point in our lives. His unhappiness and confused thinking about the kind of work he should be doing became clear when he learned he lacked the aptitudes needed to be a contented and successful engineer. His test results showed instead that he had an ideal executive aptitude pattern. He also tested very high in vocabulary, indicative of broad general knowledge. Although vocabulary is not an aptitude but is acquired, the Laboratory's testers always measure it and lay great stress on its importance because of its relationship to the successful use of our talents.

My husband was so happy and relieved over what he had learned about himself that he insisted I be tested, too. So I went to Hoboken and went through the battery of work-samples and vocabulary tests. I found it a fascinating experience. It was hard to believe that such simple tests could tell so much. When I had completed the battery, the test administrator brought me in to meet Mr. O'Connor himself, for he was to go over my test scores, tell me what they meant, and where my strongest talents lay.

In later years, Mr. O'Connor loved to tell people about our first meeting. His version was that after he had told me that I tested as a writer and urged me to write, I had asked in a trembling voice, "But what shall I write about?" He said that he had replied gleefully, "Write about the Human Engineering Laboratory!" Whether or not his memory served him accurately is beside the point, but three books and a number of articles published about the work indicate that I took his advice.

After both of us were tested, my husband and I decided to learn as much as we could about the work. We always had been extremely close but we became even more so as this knowledge of our aptitudes revealed things about each other we never really had understood. Between ourselves, we had great fun trying to figure out from their behavior the aptitudes of our friends and people with whom we had dealings. Soon an overly shy and retiring person seemed far less of a "creep" to us and became instead, in my husband's words, "A good rousing subjective." A loud, back-slapping "know-it-all" became, in the Laboratory nomenclature, a low-vocabulary objective.

But it was far more than a game with us. We were searching to find out how my husband could make the transition into executive work more suited to his aptitudes and high vocabulary. It was then that fate stepped in. War was imminent and he was called back into the Navy. We moved to Washington where he served throughout the war as a Commander with the Office of Naval Intelligence. When the war ended he went in an executive capacity with what is now the Central Intelligence Agency where he remained until his death in 1961. Here his executive talents, his better understanding of human behavior and his high vocabulary served him well both at home and abroad.

Over the years, there has been ample opportunity on a purely personal basis to see how the research of the Human Engineering Laboratory checked out in real life, not only in my husband and myself, but in our children who were first tested at the age of nine and again in their teens. We found the knowledge of inestimable value in understanding their behavior, in encouraging hobbies and interests based on their strongest aptitudes, in helping them choose high school and college courses, and also in the selection of both high school and college.

In order to write about the Laboratory I came into closer association with the staff and especially with the

O'Connors. It meant having access to files, talking with persons tested, and learning of the experience of others through hundreds of letters from my readers. The first two books were written before I went back to work which I did when our daughters went away to college. One, *Know Your Real Abilities,* was written in collaboration with my husband. The third book, of which this is an adaptation, was written and published after I had retired, to celebrate the fiftieth anniversary of the Laboratory. The text of all three books was read and approved by Mr. O'Connor before publication. While I was working and doing a totally different kind of writing I still maintained a strong relationship with the Laboratory, attending annual meetings as a trustee and member. I never was employed or paid by the Laboratory, however.

Knowing the O'Connors intimately for so many years was to me a rare privilege. When my husband was alive we made a most compatible foursome. After I was widowed they came to my home in Washington even more frequently, and I often was a guest in their home wherever they were living, whether it happened to be in their permanent home in Boston, or temporary ones in New York, California or Mexico. They traveled extensively, always taking their work with them. Mrs. O'Connor gave faithful help in writing letters, taking notes, and compiling research materials. They were together in Mexico where they had been testing the aptitudes of primitive Zapotec Indians when both became sick and died in 1973.

To anyone who ever knew them they were an unforgettable couple. In appearance alone they made a striking pair. He was small and dark with graying hair and a little Van Dyke beard and with kind but penetrating brown eyes. She was petite, erect, with beautifully coiffed snow white hair, vivacious and charming. Not only had she been a distinguished architect in Boston, but she also taught until well in her eighties. Young people adored this couple, for they were so adaptable, so completely ageless in outlook and humor. With this was an air of dignity and a charming grace and elegance that merged with vitality and wit. They dressed for dinner every night no matter where they were, even if they cooked and served dinner themselves. The walls of their brownstone Boston home were covered with Chinese tea chest papers, and all four floors were filled with antiques and art objects collected from countries around the world. Books were everywhere and they always were learning something new, even foreign languages. As a pioneer in uncovering the importance of vocabulary, Mr. O'Connor built what is probably the most complete collection of dictionaries in the world.

In spite of his many interests, the unfolding of knowledge of human behavior and through this the increase of personal happiness was the one thing to which he was completely dedicated throughout his long life, and he worked at it endlessly and tirelessly. Fortunately over the years he had developed a highly competent and superb staff throughout the country who continue to carry on the work with much the same dedication, purpose and capability, so that his legacy to us lives on, growing continually.

Johnson O'Connor was convinced that it is the aptitudes we have and don't use that underlie restlessness and frustration, that they are born with us and constantly importune us for outlet and development. He would agree with Thomas Wolfe who wrote in his book, *The Web and the Rock*, "If a man has a talent and cannot use it, he has failed. If he has a talent and uses only half of it, he has partly failed. If he has a talent and somehow learns to use the whole of it, he has gloriously succeeded, and won satisfaction and triumph few men ever know."

Many of us probably have talents we don't know we have, buried deep, layered over with acquired skills and disguised by the tendency so many of us have to imitate others rather than to be ourselves. And contrary to popular belief, a college education may not always be the answer for all of us. In some cases, forcing a person to go to college may be counterproductive if not even destructive. We may also, in fact, be training so many professionals there will not be enough jobs to go around. A knowledge of real abilities is particularly important for it gives clues to more choices in the way we might go. What the human engineers have uncovered so far is knowledge that can help us lay a course in our work, in our hobbies, and in our daily living so that we can come closer to achieving that intangible something which almost everyone would like to get from life.

M.B.

1.

Discovering Aptitudes

Because many persons never have heard of the Human Engineering Laboratory and many are skeptical of aptitude tests *per se,* it is important first of all to give you some of its background and how it all came about.

In 1922, Johnson O'Connor headed the engineering department of a General Electric Company plant in West Lynn, Massachusetts. O'Connor was a young, brilliant philosophy graduate from Harvard who had worked as assistant to Percival Lowell in astronomical mathematical research. Because he wanted to learn more about engineering, he started at General Electric as a factory worker, but soon was put in charge of engineering. Here he worked under the plant manager, Mr. F. P. Cox, who actually was responsible for starting the Laboratory.

Cox and O'Connor first attempted to reduce overall costs by increasing the efficiency of the workers. It seemed to them that if people did work that was both natural and right to them, not only would this compatibility (rightness) boost efficiency but it would make them take a greater interest in their jobs. The jobs themselves would have to be examined and worksamples (tests) for each would have to be used. At that time little or nothing had been done with aptitude testing and the chief evaluation of personnel came from intelligence test scores. After a long study, both men decided that there was too much guesswork in this method. Intelligence scores needed to be interpreted to reveal the requisite aptitudes for each profession. What Cox and O'Connor wanted never had been done, so they decided to do it themselves.

Mr. O'Connor knew that in the past six thousand years little progress had been made in understanding the true nature of humans. On the other hand, the development of physics and chemistry in the last hundred years had greatly influenced industrial progress. During that time no one had tried to apply to the understanding of people and their natural abilities the research techniques of physics and chemistry. It seemed to Mr. O'Connor that scientifically measuring many persons in different occupations would show the mental traits characteristic of the most successful people. If these traits were isolated by devising reliable measures for them, then these traits could be synthesized into work patterns that should help people understand themselves and what they could do best because it was natural to them. Gerard Swope, the General Electric president, agreed to the revolutionary idea and suggested the title "human engineering."

Then began the long and difficult task of devising tests or worksamples. Some revealed what the HEL wanted to know; others were scrapped after repeated trials. Participation in the worksamples was voluntary but the employees quizzed were interested and nearly all of the three thousand who signed up for them participated. One of the first worksamples was for measuring finger dexterity in meter assembly. This worksample proved easy, and in a few months the tests located eight girls faster in finger dexterity than any trained operator. Next came a worksample for observation as a test for choosing inspectors. This seemed important since an inspector does nothing but look and one never knows if he really sees what he is looking for. By selecting persons who scored high in observation for inspector jobs, quality control was improved and thus complaints from customers fell off significantly.

2

As time went on and more worksamples were developed and more persons were tested, the human engineers found they were going beyond the scope of industrial efficiency. The aptitude measurements had been geared to the job to be filled; now, after a few years, the point of view was reversed to considering first the individual and his aptitudes and then to placing him in the job best suited to his abilites.

Word about what was going on began to get around. Employees wanted their children tested; other business firms wanted testing done. Outside demands became so pressing that Mr. O'Connor began administering the worksamples evenings and weekends in his home, devoting some time, too, to giving the tests in colleges. In 1928 he went to London to study the problem of human relations under the Wertheim Fellowship from Harvard. Technical colleges were especially interested in the work, and for three years it was carried on at Massachusetts Institute of Technology, and then for about a dozen years at Stevens Institute of Technology where Harvey N. Davis, the president, was keenly interested in promoting the work. Human engineers were given a fellowship and could apply their work toward a master's degree.

In the meantime, a Laboratory had been set up in Boston and Chicago in conjunction with what is now the Illinois Institute of Technology.

The Laboratory was dedicated to the isolation and measurement of inborn traits and their relationship to behavior and occupation. Aptitudes are believed to be inherited and fixed at birth. To date, the Laboratory has isolated nineteen aptitudes and can measure them with remarkable accuracy; many others are still being investigated. Combinations of these inborn traits form work patterns that HEL believe characterize persons most successful in their fields.

The nineteen aptitudes and the tests or worksamples for them which the Laboratory has discovered are:

1. *Personality*—the objective personality works best with others; the subjective belongs in specialized, individual work. The test employs a free association or free response

3

format. The administrator says a word and the examinee immediately responds with the first word he thinks of. In each personality worksample the administrator uses 100 words to stimulate answers.

2. *Graphoria*—clerical ability, adeptness at paperwork and dealing with figures and symbols. The examinee is presented with a sheet of paper in the center of which are two columns of digits separated by a short line. He must put a check on the line between each pair of identical digits only. As the worksample progresses, the size of the numbers increases.

3. *Ideaphoria*—or creative imagination—fluency of ideas. The examinee is presented with an imaginary topic, such as, "What would you do, and what do you think others should do if one week from today the sun were to go out?" He is told to write just as much as he can as fast as possible on this topic for ten minutes.

4. *Structural visualization*—Ability to think in three dimensions, to visualize solids. Abstract visualization is the ability to deal in ideas. Lack of structural visualization means you have abstract visualization. In one worksample, the wiggly block, the examinee is shown a six-piece wooden block. It is taken apart and the pieces are put in front of him at random. He then assembles it as quickly as he can. If successful, he is given a nine-piece block to assemble and then a twelve-piece one.

Another worksample consists of a set of wooden blocks, some sides of which are painted black. The examinee must assemble the blocks to form a cube ($3 \times 3 \times 3$ blocks) which is black on the six exterior surfaces but not on any interior surface. One of the blocks has no black surfaces.

Abstract visualization is not measured directly but rather is inferred from the examinee's performance in structural visualization. If he scores high, he is given a low score in abstract visualization; if low in structural visualization he is given a high score in abstract visualization.

5. *Inductive reasoning*—ability to form a logical conclusion from scattered facts. The examinee is shown a group of pictures, some of which have something in common. He is asked to check those pictures which he feels are related. He does

this for sixty groups of pictures, working as quickly as he can. The speed and accuracy with which the relationships are discovered afford a good measure of inductive reasoning.

6. *Analytical reasoning*—ability to resolve an idea into its component parts. The examinee is given the information in a random sequence and must arrange it systematically as quickly as he can. No writing is involved.

7. *Finger dexterity*—ability to manipulate fingers skillfully. This worksample consists of a board containing 100 holes and a number of pins. Working as fast as he can, the examinee must put three pins in each hole.

8. *Tweezer dexterity*—ability to handle small tools easily. The examinee must transfer 100 small pins, moving each from one hole to another, using a set of tweezers. The worksample is timed and scored on both speed and accuracy.

9. *Observation*—ability to take careful notice. This worksample consists of a standard photograph of a number of household objects and ten comparison photographs where at least one change has been made. The examinee first studies the standard photograph for a minute, then it is taken away and the first comparison photograph is shown. The examinee must name the changes he observes in the comparison photograph. When this has been done he is shown the standard photograph for ten seconds, then he observes the second comparison photograph and names the changes. This procedure is repeated until all ten comparisons have been shown.

10. *Design memory*—ability to memorize designs readily. The examinee sees a simple dot and line design for a short time. Then it is removed and he is told to reproduce it as accurately as he can. This procedure is repeated with nine more designs of increasing complexity.

11. *Tonal memory*—ability to remember sounds, an ear for music. Two series of notes are presented in quick succession. The two series are identical except that one note in the second series has been changed. The examinee must decide which of the notes has been changed and write the number of the note on his worksample sheet. As the worksample progresses the number of notes in each series increases,

presenting a greater challenge to the examinee's tonal memory.

12. *Pitch discrimination*—ability to differentiate musical tones, a trait needed in playing a musical instrument whose pitch is not set. Two electronically reproduced "beeps" are presented in quick succession. The second "beep" is higher or lower in cycles per second. The examinee must decide whether the second tone is higher or lower and mark "H" or "L" on his worksample sheet. As the worksample progresses the difference between the "beeps" gradually decreases to present more challenge to the examinee's pitch discrimination.

13. *Rhythmic ability*—ability to keep time, a trait needed to play drums. Two series of notes are presented in rapid succession. The rhythm of the second series differs by one note from that of the first. The examinee must decide which note has the different rhythm and mark it on his worksheet.

14. *Timbre discrimination*—ability to distinguish sounds of the same pitch and volume from each other. Two notes are presented in quick succession, alike in pitch and duration but sometimes different in tone quality. The examinee must decide whether the second note is the same or different and mark it on his worksheet.

15. *Number memory*—ability to remember numbers of all kinds, to keep many things in your mind. The examinee is shown a six-digit number for one second. Then following a short pause another and different six-digit number is shown. This procedure is repeated until he has seen eight separate six-digit numbers for one second each. Then he repeats aloud as many of the six-digit numbers as he can recall. The same numbers are again presented to him in a different order, after which he again repeats aloud all of them he can recall. This procedure is repeated twice more with the same numbers in a different order each time.

16. *Proportional appraisal*—ability to discern harmonious proportions. This worksample is composed of thirty-six plates, each of which shows four similar objects. The examinee is asked to select the best of each four and rank the others in their order of excellence.

17. *Silograms*—test for ability to learn languages, ease in remembering unfamiliar words, technical jargon, etc. The examinee is shown a pair of words, one a nonsense word, the other an English one. After 3.6 seconds, another pair of words is presented. This procedure is repeated until the examinee has seen twenty different nonsense/English pairs. He is then given a list of the twenty nonsense words and is asked to write in the correct English word next to each one. This procedure is repeated three more times with the same nonsense/English pairs presented in differing orders.

18. *Foresight*—ability to look ahead, concern or prudence about the future. There are two variations of this work-sample. In the first, the examinee looks at a simple line drawing and names as many objects as possible which the drawing brings to mind within 45 seconds. This procedure is repeated nine times with a different line drawing shown each time. In the second variation, the only difference is that the stimuli are more complex drawings.

19. *Color perception*—the ability to distinguish colors. Lack of this aptitude means color blindness. This aptitude is measured by a series of colored slides shown to the examinee for a few seconds each. Each slide contains a number or word embedded in colored dots which can be seen only by persons with color perception. Color blindness is a genetically determined characteristic.

Other important traits measured by the Laboratory but which do not fit the description of an aptitude include eye dominance, which indicates whether you are right or left sided and should use the corresponding hand; grip, which indicates physical energy; taste, which indicates your ability to taste a sour substance; and vocabulary.

Through self analysis it may be possible to discover your own aptitudes. For example, if you enjoy and are good at mechanical and scientific problems, if objects interest you more than abstract ideas, you may have structural visualization; if you can see quickly a common thread in seemingly unrelated facts, or even like to argue, you may have inductive reasoning; and so on. But you can't always be certain, for you can't really test yourself accurately any more than holding a scalpel in your hand will make you a surgeon. Of course there are some who know instinctively their aptitude strong points and shortcomings, who know what they want to do in life and go ahead and do it. But for those who aren't certain, who are plagued with doubts, testing by the Human Engineering Laboratory may give revealing solutions to personal problems.

Many industrial firms and schools, as well as individuals, wanted testing done. The time had come to branch out, to set up Laboratories in other localities to service more persons and, at the same time, to provide a greater cross-section of people for research purposes. The original HEL was incorporated as a non-profit educational and scientific research organization. It now has twelve offices in the United States and one in Mexico. These are in New York, Boston, Tulsa, Philadelphia, Chicago, Washington, Detroit, Los Angeles, San Diego, Atlanta, Fort Worth, Houston, and Mexico City. Other locations are in the planning stage. Some are called the Human Engineering Laboratory. In the near future all will be called the Johnson O'Connor Research Foundation.

The information comes from measuring aptitudes—more than one-half million people have taken the tests—and from extensive follow-up studies. The Laboratory is not a vocational guidance group, but a non-profit scientific research organization. Anyone tested, although he learns vital facts about himself and directions to pursue, is in a sense a guinea pig for human understanding research.

These half million people whom the Laboratory has tested represent all ages and all walks of life, from students to dishwashers to famous entertainers, presidents of large corporations, even a President of the United States. In all the testing, one significant factor stands out: aptitudes know no economic or racial barrier. Nor does it make any difference if you are successful or unsuccessful, educated or uneducated. Aptitudes appear in all kinds of people, and it is the rare person who doesn't have at least a few strong aptitudes upon which he can build a satisfying life if he gives to their development hard work and the acquisition of skill and knowledge.

The Laboratory has found that not using aptitudes causes restlessness and frustration. Our inborn aptitudes constantly need development and outlet. The HEL also stresses measuring vocabulary, an acquired, not innate, trait. The Laboratory has found in any occupation studied that a large vocabulary, which indicates a broad, general knowledge, invariably characterizes the most successful persons. By knowing our true aptitudes and vocabulary, we can come closer to fulfilling our hopes in life.

The purpose of this book is to show how these aptitudes are utilized in different kinds of work and how they affect your behavior not only in work but in other aspects of daily living. I have written *Your Natural Gifts* in the hope that knowledge of what the human engineers have discovered might give you greater understanding of yourself and others, whether you are tested or not. I use many case histories to show what others have done, for often we can identify with another person's problem and see clues to the answer to our own. Since the Laboratory's records are confidential, I can reveal no names of persons tested, although the temptation is great for some are nationally known.

Getting Pleasure from Your Job

Most of us hold jobs for most of our lives. Yet how many of us really enjoy our work and gain from it a feeling of accomplishment, confidence, personal fulfillment and serenity? We would agree with Thomas Carlyle when he wrote, "Blessed is he who has found his work; let him ask no other blessedness." Work unlocks our creative forces; it gives us at least some understanding of ourselves. If you feel frustrated and restless in your job, the cause may well be unused aptitudes. Each unused aptitude begets a restlessness and a discontent as we are not using these inner strengths. We have a vague sense of wasting our lives.

The truth is you probably are far more talented than you realize. The human engineers have found that most of those tested have at least eight or nine high aptitudes, but use only three or four in their jobs. Some use none at all, relying chiefly on acquired skills but never getting very far ahead. We have only to look at the griping and grumbling that goes on in almost any office to realize the personal frustrations that so often seethe beneath the surface.

Some people, by using only a few aptitudes and by building the requisite skill and knowledge, forge ahead to high-paid jobs and added responsibilities which give a certain amount of satisfaction. But many, not using enough of their high abilities, exist in a state of deferred living, dreaming of a misty future when they fulfill their secret hopes. Yet they have only nebulous ideas of what they want. Still others go through the motions of their jobs and live only for evenings, weekends and vacations.

But no job is perfect. No matter how successful we are or how many aptitudes we are using, everyone has feelings of doubt, of inferiority, of disgust and boredom with what he is doing. But we have fewer of those days if we use and develop our natural talents. And most of us need to get away from our work to gain perspective and add variety to living. A recent Laboratory study found that those in staid, secure jobs tend to pursue exciting hobbies or competitive sports, while those in dangerous or insecure jobs chose quiet hobbies, such as reading, art and music.

Most of us have to earn a living and it would be nonsense to say that money is not important. We generally have financial responsibilities that come first and we also want to buy and do the things money makes possible. Furthermore, our success is often measured in the eyes of the world by the money we earn.

But we need more reward than money; we need the satisfaction of using our aptitudes too. And all aptitudes are important; each affects our behavior. For adjustment to our work, however, some aptitudes are especially crucial to the type of work we do. For example, graphoria, or accounting and clerical aptitude, is essential if one's job involves much paperwork or dealing with figures. The stenographer, accountant and banker need graphoria. Actually, it is something we use all our lives—keeping accounts, balancing checkbooks, computing income tax, and so on. The wife who snarls up the household accounts probably has low graphoria.

Unless your job involves much mathematical calculation and paperwork that you must perform yourself, having the aptitude is not so important. Executives, for example, have others to do this work for them. But where the aptitude is truly important is during school years when the groundwork is being laid for holding a future job. It takes the youngster with low graphoria a long time to do any kind of paperwork and usually he is a slow reader. It can take him five hours to do what the high graphoria student can finish in an hour. The work is distasteful to him, and unless he forces himself to do it he falls behind, and may either drop out of school or get such poor grades no college will take him. Graphoria has no relationship to intelligence and many gifted and brilliant persons lack the aptitude.

The Laboratory tests show to many students that low graphoria is the root of many of their school troubles. A high vocabulary helps to compensate for inaptitude, as do various techniques to get schoolwork done, which will be described later. Although the low graphoria person must work hard for his education, he can be cheered by the knowledge that once formal schooling is completed, he can achieve success by using his other aptitudes and let someone else do the paperwork.

Personality is another important factor for job suitability. The objective person is outgoing; he needs and likes people and enjoys working with others. The subjective person is his opposite: he likes to work alone, wrapped up in himself and his task. The objective person tends to conform, the subjective to be individualistic. Objective persons act more or less alike; each subjective person is different, unique.

Perhaps some of the greatest misfits in the working world are the subjectives in objective jobs and the objectives in subjective ones. Many subjectives find objective behavior annoying, and objectives sense a lack of communication with the subjectives. In general, however, the objective person has the easier time. Because he is outgoing, he is not so sensitive to criticism and rebuffs; he can slough off many matters that could burn the ego of the extremely subjective person deeply. The human engineers believe that the subjective has the greater problem for his thoughts center on himself. Unless he has some specialty utilizing his true aptitudes, a speciality he can excel in and pursue with a singleness of purpose, he can be the most wretched of all persons —a prime candidate for many mental and emotional disturbances. On the other hand, it is the subjectives who become the leaders, who make the greater contribution to the world, who achieve true greatness.

You may wonder how a person could be drawn into work inappropriate for his personality. It would seem that he would avoid it instinctively. Often he does, but all too often he does not. The reasons are many, but frequently they can be traced to background and the influence of family and friends. Deeply ingrained feelings of inferiority or shyness can push an objective youth into subjective pursuits; a sense of duty in carrying on family traditions or fulfilling parental desires can be another cause. And school success frequently underlies the subjective going into objective work, for often the subjective student becomes the school leader, the one who is voted most likely to succeed, and, as the class idol, is much admired and praised. It is natural for a subjective person to dramatize himself in a situation—actors and actresses are extremely subjective. What he really is doing is acting a part. Everyone tells him he should be a big executive or a supersalesman, that with his personality and leadership he could make a fortune in business. If he follows this advice, too often he learns the bitter truth.

The Laboratory's worksample test for personality seems simple, but to the individual its findings can spell the difference between adjustment and maladjustment both in work and in personal life. The worksample is a word association test developed from one first created by Kent and Rosanoff and has proved to be highly reliable. The test administrator reads a list of one hundred words and you respond to each with the first word that pops into your mind. If you have an objective personality, most of your answers are general and impersonal; if you are subjective, the majority of your responses have a personal association.

Anyone older than nine can take the worksamples —the Laboratory has even tested persons in their eighties. It strongly recommends, however, that young persons be tested so that parents can encourage their natural bent and get them started in a suitable direction in their education.

The Laboratory says that three-quarters of the world

is objective and the other quarter subjective. Where we score on the personality scale indicates the general type of work we should do to be in tune with our basic nature. The extremely objective person belongs in such work as selling; the objective in executive or similar group-oriented work; the subjective in the professions; and the extremely subjective in more cloistered, individual work such as research, or the creative and performing arts. Those who score on the border of the two personalities can do objective work, but the human engineers believe that as a safeguard they should consider themselves subjective and develop a specialty. From long experience in measuring aptitudes, and extensive followup studies of persons first tested twenty and thirty years ago, the Laboratory is convinced more than ever of the need to follow the dictates of our true personality, that it is vital not only for success in work but for personal contentment.

Another significant aptitude is structural visualization. This ability to think in three dimensions, to visualize solids clearly, is essential to the engineer, surgeon, scientist, dentist, architect, sculptor, mechanic, carpenter, and the like. For example, no one ever has seen an atom nucleus, but a scientist must be able to see its structure in his mind. We are living in an age where structural visualization is important, where there is much emphasis on scientific achievement and many opportunities in structural fields. Many people are drawn mistakenly into a profession requiring structural visualization. But without the aptitude you never can compete successfully with those who have it, nor can you derive satisfaction in the work. An interest in working with your hands, which could mean strong hand dexterities and not structural visualization ability, often misleads some into structural fields. So does interest in general science, which actually is history and involves inductive reasoning rather than structural visualization.

The human engineers test many sons who have grown up with the idea of following in their father's footsteps as surgeons, engineers, or other structural careers, despite having difficulty as their preparatory courses become more advanced. Invariably, these sons lack the aptitude. Structural visualization is a sex-linked recessive trait, passing from mother to son, never from father to son. A daughter receives the aptitude from either her father or mother.

The Laboratory administers a number of worksamples to measure structural visualization. Perhaps the best known is the wiggly block, devised by Mr. O'Connor, the Laboratory founder. This block is cut into wavy pieces that you are asked to fit together to form the solid block. The person high in the aptitude assembles the block quickly. One well-known executive became so exasperated with the block that he threw it out the window.

A low score in structural visualization indicates what the human engineers term abstract visualization, the ability to deal with abstract ideas. They believe that true aptitudes are inherited in pairs and that the lack of a trait means you possess an opposite ability. In the case of structural visualization the aptitude is abstract visualization. Briefly, the high structure person is most interested in things and problem solving, and the high abstract in ideas and people. The best executives, lawyers, teachers, salesmen, writers, painters, actors and musicians score low in structural visualization.

You might call structural visualization a man's aptitude, for only 25 per cent of women have it. Most work that uses the aptitude naturally calls for a subjective personality as it requires long study and research. The objective person strong in the aptitude has a difficult problem, for beyond such work as architecture, construction and city planning, the possibilities for combining the two in work are limited. And the aptitude is a strong and basic one that demands use if its possessor is to achieve any kind of inner peace. Suitable fields for the objective personality involve working with people and ideas and, while the objective person is drawn naturally to working with people, strong structural visualization not only stands in his way in dealing with abstract ideas, but he too often gets little or no opportunity to use the aptitude. The human engineers have found that manufacturing executives with high structural visualization and objective personalities usually resign from the big corporations between the ages of thirty-five and fifty. Their unused structural visualization ability makes them restless and dissatisfied. Mr. O'Connor believed that such persons do not belong in large corporations, but should start their own business in a structural field.

All unused aptitudes, as much as inaptitude, hinder being comfortable, being ourselves, in our work. Once we know our inborn abilities, we can take positive steps to shift gradually out of work that requires aptitudes we lack. This is not easy, for it requires patience and hard work. It is something we must do for ourselves, but it can be done and is worth the effort. Each aptitude we bring to our work gives us more satisfaction and also aids our progress.

Our vocabulary level plays an important part too, for if it varies too greatly from that of our associates or objectives, we never can feel that we really belong. It is important to build vocabulary, both general and job-related. We can have every aptitude, but without a good vocabulary, vocational knowledge and skill, our aptitudes will get us nowhere. To get the most satisfaction from using our aptitudes, and to give meaning to our work, we need to direct our efforts toward a goal that will keep us busy and interested throughout life.

3

Setting a Goal

The constant pursuit of the impossible dream, of a distant goal that we never can quite reach, fills life with meaning and challenge. In later years we can look back with satisfaction and ahead with pleasure to more challenges and interests. We have only to pause a minute to realize that the persons we most admire throughout history, and to whom we feel a sense of gratitude, are those who were dedicated to helping make the world a better place. Each according to his talents, beliefs, and interests contributed to mankind— perhaps through science, philosophy, art, music, literature or humanitarian efforts. And while we remember only the great names, the help of countless others was needed to make impossible dreams come true.

Our goal in life must be chosen in keeping with our true aptitudes. But for lasting satisfaction, this goal should benefit not only ourselves, but others. The speed and ease of modern transportation and communication make it easy to find many challenging opportunities to make the world a better place. The Laboratory's engineers advise young persons tested to think first in terms of solving some broad world problem rather than of becoming a doctor, lawyer, businessman, teacher, or the like; next to consider getting the education or experience suitable for their aptitudes and necessary for working toward their goal. War, poverty, world health, education, ecology, race relations, government and law are only some of the problems upon which to work. Nor does this program obviate a business career, for business itself is attempting more and more world problem-solving.

Many of the problems are old, but they are of more pressing concern to us now than ever before. When this country was young and raw, building a new nation was often goal enough. But the vanishing of the frontier has meant population pressure and economic catastrophes unknown in the last century. During the 1930's depression most people wanted only to get a job—anything to avoid selling apples on the street. After World War II, people were kept busy just keeping pace with technological changes. But, as everyone knows, few young people now are engrossed with economic conditions, yet they are dissatisfied with today's world situation. We have enough material goods; consequently, values are turning from the materialistic to the spiritual.

It is significant that increasing numbers of college graduates are going into low-paying, social service-oriented careers. Youth always has been idealistic, and perhaps we should take more seriously the hopes and dreams we have at that age if such dreams are not mere chimeras or wishful thinking. Young people need guidance about their real aptitudes so that they can work in the right direction and formulate specific goals. As Thoreau said, "If you have built castles in the air, your work need not be lost; that is where they should be; now put foundations under them."

These foundations need to be built solidly and intelligently, by means of true aptitudes, skill and knowledge. This building takes time and effort. Youth may want to hurry, but as Dr. Samuel Johnson said, "He who wants to do a great deal at once will never do anything." The path to a big goal is reached by a series of lesser immediate personal goals, and each is a small step ahead. While earning a living may seem unrelated to the ultimate objective, it helps one move forward toward a goal.

Setting a goal is far easier for the person who is strong

in the aptitude of foresight than for the person who lacks it. In explaining what the aptitude means, Mr. O'Connor said, "We have long suspected that foresight measured and revealed the capacity for personal value judgments and [it is] a measure of persistence, a mixture of the capacity to foresee distant goals and objectives and to relate these goals to one's immediate needs and requirements, and yet at the same time [to] recognize their future personal, social or economic worth."

The person low in foresight often abandons things on impulse and then regrets doing so. He may leave college suddenly because at the moment he can't see its future value. He may sell a business when it is just about to make an upswing and then watch it prosper under someone else. He may quit a job just when he is in line for a promotion. He rarely finishes graduate study, for pursuing this distant goal demands seeing its ultimate value. For those who want to go to college, the Laboratory believes in a liberal arts four-year college background as a foundation for later life and for graduate work if it is desired or indicated by aptitudes or profession. With today's demand for specific knowledge, graduate school can be an important help in getting a worthwhile job and in working toward a goal. But the low-foresight person rarely can be persuaded to do this. He thinks further schooling a waste of time, for he can't see its future worth.

The low-foresight person may require and want a goal beyond the immediate future, and often needs some outside urging to seek one. As Mr. O'Connor said, "For the low-foresight person, who at heart craves the distant goal, as much as for those who score high, some insignificant immediate difficulty looms great, like a small object so near that it obscures the world. At such a moment, the low foresight person needs only a word of encouragement to persist, and without it too often gives up just short of success."

A typical example of this is a man tested recently at the Philadelphia laboratory who wanted to quit a top position in a large company. He felt he was wasting his time and wanted to do something to improve education. He tested as suitable for his work but with low foresight. In reality, he had not seen the opportunities within his own company which recently had embarked on an extensive employee educational program important enough to receive rather wide publicity. The test administrator, having read about the program, mentioned it to the man who knew about it, but had never connected it with himself. When it was pointed out to him that he was in a position to play a part in the program, he decided to stay where he was.

The human engineers interpret foresight as a personal thing, not like predicting the stock market or planning ahead in business. One man, tested recently in Los Angeles, had been vice-president of a large food company. In a moment of discouragement, he had quit his job. When he came to the Laboratory he had been out of work for four years. He scored as an executive, but with very low foresight. He insisted this score could not be true. To prove it, he listed for the test administrator all the things he had planned for his company. But this is business and not personal foresight. He could have stayed on his job, but he hadn't foreseen his difficulties in finding a comparable job, particularly at middle-age and after quitting a top job on impulse. His wife agreed that he had no personal foresight and remarked bluntly that "He never could see beyond the end of his nose."

We can have great foresight, but unless our goal and our pursuit of it coincide with our aptitudes, our efforts can be futile. Our wishful thinking cannot come true. A twenty-eight-year-old man who came for testing was a recent example. He was enthusiastic about his decision to practice international law; he felt much needed to be done and he wanted to be a part of it. He had saved his money and was planning to go back to school to study law. He scored high in foresight, objective in personality, and strong in aptitudes for art and music, but he lacked the inductive reasoning ability which he would need greatly for law. The best lawyers are subjective, a trait needed for the long hours of isolated study. When his insuitability for law was pointed out to him, he was disappointed at first, but gradually began to see the logic. He admitted he always had been keenly interested in art and music despite no background in either. Since he had executive aptitudes and art and music ability, he decided to get training in the latter and aim for an executive job in a branch of the performing arts, with a goal of improving them.

In setting a goal, vocabulary becomes increasingly necessary and important. Even if we have high foresight, with low vocabulary we don't know enough to see our own possibilities, nor to grasp the concepts of what a long-term, problem-solving goal involves. Nor can we progress far enough in our work to work effectively toward a goal. Fortunately, vocabulary is acquired, and not inborn, so anyone can build one with work. The Laboratory tests so many who are held back by low vocabulary, despite brilliant aptitudes, that it cannot emphasize too strongly the importance of vocabulary building. And it has seen so many instances where vocabulary growth has resulted not only in progress at work, but in opening whole new horizons of interest and understanding.

Albert Einstein said: "Try not to become a man of success but rather try to become a man of value." By using and developing our aptitudes and raising our vocabulary to higher levels, and directing our efforts toward a useful goal, we can gain not only lasting satisfaction but have a better chance of following his advice.

4

The Importance of Vocabulary

Today's frontier is knowledge. Brain has taken precedence over brawn; our physical struggle for existence has been replaced by intellectual struggle, and a knowledge of words has become a most valuable tool. The more vocabulary we possess, the more efficient are these tools of thought. With a good vocabulary, which indicates scope of knowledge, we can grasp the thoughts of others and be able to communicate our own thoughts to them.

As early as the 1930's, the HEL found a close relationship between a large, precise knowledge of English words and achievement in life. Worldly success, earnings and management status correlated with vocabulary scores. In follow-up studies of persons tested as much as twenty or thirty years ago, a limited vocabulary is proving an important factor in holding men and women back from achieving the position which their aptitudes showed they should have gained. The truth is that low vocabulary decreases the effectiveness of inborn gifts in any civilization.

Youth, with its idealism and enthusiasm, probably has always wanted to change the world. Perhaps there is only more evidence of this desire today. But those with limited vocabulary never can alter the world.

Frustration about inability to express thoughts in words too often results in physical aggressiveness. It is interesting to note that the Laboratory has found that the nation's vocabulary level has been decreasing one point a year for some years, while crime has been increasing. Strong aptitudes and low vocabulary can spell trouble. This is especially true for those with high inductive reasoning. One in nine teenagers scores high in inductive reasoning but low vocabulary. With high vocabulary and inductive reasoning, law, diplomacy, editorial work and government can be outlets. Without vocabulary, the same aptitude gropes angrily for ideal forms of government, social justice and reforms, and finds expression in violence, protestations, and rebellions of many kinds in an attempt to realize hopes envisioned by this strong aptitude.

For any individual, a low vocabulary is a serious handicap. Ambitious and energetic persons can push ahead in their jobs just so far, but then they reach a plateau caused by low vocabulary. They never advance. And while youthful zest and high aptitudes can enable us to forge ahead despite low vocabulary, when we become mature the world expects us to know something and we are judged on knowledge rather than our possibilities. The world doesn't see our aptitudes, but it pays for knowledge because that can be seen. There is a relationship between the length of time a man stays with a job and his aptitudes, the money he makes, and vocabulary. Laboratory studies show that at middle-age the low-vocabulary persons are stuck in routine jobs. Furthermore, when big companies have their shakedowns and mergers, too often the low-vocabulary persons find themselves out on the street. Too often they place the blame on prejudice, inside politics, and personal antagonism when the truth can be traced to low vocabulary. One man had earned a fat salary salvaging nearly bankrupt organizations, bringing them to a point where less talented men could carry on the work. He was forty-two when he came to the Chicago Laboratory to take the tests. The tests themselves were a gift, for he was out of work and dependent on friends for support. He had brilliant aptitudes, but scored at the bottom in English vocabulary. Starting work when he was in his twenties, on the strength of strong aptitudes and unusual vitality he had tackled and solved complex problems of decrepit corporations which others could not seem to do. But aptitudes decline with age, the age of decline differing with each aptitude. Inductive reasoning, for example, declines at age twenty-three, ideaphoria at thirty-one, and the declines should be offset by vocabulary gains.

Mr. O'Connor pointed out, "Any man or woman who succeeds in work and in life by the application of extraordinary aptitudes alone, by the use of brilliant inherent ability, begins to lose standing soon after thirty, and by forty sinks noticeably. If at thirty or thirty-five, accumulated knowledge of the English language, is below the born aptitudes on which one has depended for success, performance deteriorates, not suddenly, but gradually, at first almost imperceptibly, until it declines to the level of one's vocabulary." On the other hand, he said, "If sometime after thirty, when aptitudes start down, but English vocabulary is as high as the aptitudes one has been using, knowledge picks up, offsets weaker aptitudes and the world sees no decline in performance."

For the above mentioned individual his low vocabulary was at fault. But like similar persons, he blamed the outside world for his failure, for not appreciating his achievements. He was resentful that he was not made president of one of the companies he had rebuilt. But the human engineers have found that presidents and vice-presidents average higher in vocabulary than any other group tested—higher than lawyers, professors, doctors, scientists, writers, or others one would assume would be at the top.

The encouraging fact is that there always is hope for the low-vocabulary person since vocabulary is acquired and not innate. Expanding a vocabulary may be somewhat easier for the person who scores high in the language learning aptitude (silograms) because of a natural ability to learn and remember unfamiliar words. But the Laboratory has developed ways for anybody to build vocabulary rapidly at any age. Evaluation of artificially-acquired vocabulary shows no difference from one gained otherwise.

If you have high-vocabulary parents, you have a head

start, for children of such parents almost always score high vocabulary, but not as high as their parents. Our vocabulary grows faster in our first year of life than in any other period. This, of course, is a thinking and not a speaking vocabulary. At about age ten it improves twice as fast as a few years later, and three times as fast as when we reach college age. But the Laboratory has found that vocabulary test scores rarely improve because of formal schooling, and for this reason it urges parents to encourage vocabulary building at an early age. This is extremely important, for a limited vocabulary leads directly to school and classroom troubles, and often college rejection or subsequent college failure. All this can leave a young person with strong feelings of failure and inferiority, and a lack of inner confidence that may have lasting consequences.

Building a large and exact English vocabulary does not seem so formidable when we realize we already know a great many words, and that only about 3,500 words separate the high-vocabulary person from the low. Yet these 3,500 words can mean the difference between success and failure. The word order of English is, of course, Anglo-Saxon, but the words that give subtlety and precision are Latin. Even though Latin is being dropped in school, the human engineers have found that the number of years of Latin study correlates with a large and exact English vocabulary which in turn correlates with earnings.

But building vocabulary does not mean the acquisition of a smattering of spectacular words that we can throw out casually in conversation in an attempt to impress others. After fifty years of research, the Laboratory has formulated three laws of vocabulary learning that enable one to build a permanent, exact vocabulary, and not merely an assortment of fancy words that soon are forgotten.

The first law is that English words can be arranged in order of difficulty, that every word studied belongs somewhere on a scale that extends from the well-known to the almost unknown. If everyone in the country knows the meaning of a word it is easy; if few know the meaning of a word it is hard. The order of difficulty is based on calculating the percentage of people who know the word and arranging words in the order of that percentage. Even though the Midwest scores lower in vocabulary than the East, the order of words is exactly the same.

The second law is that our English vocabulary stops rather suddenly on the familiarity scale. Up to this borderline, we know most of the English words that exist, but beyond that very few. A difficult word beyond this boundary may be memorized but is soon forgotten.

The third law is that our rate of learning is greatest just at the boundary of our vocabulary level. Thus, in building vocabulary we need to begin at our borderline and work up from there, making sure each word is learned and understood thoroughly. The technique is to learn words in sequence, not at random. If a word is beyond one's present knowledge, it is not really understood and is soon forgotten. As Goethe said, "Whatever you cannot understand, you cannot possess." But the word for which one is ready becomes at once a working part of one's vocabulary. This order of difficulty does not apply to the foreigner learning English, for he learns first those words derived from his own language.

Vocabulary can also be improved by good reading which certainly adds to knowledge. But as we read we should keep a dictionary at hand to look up the words we don't know, and not just guess at their meanings. Some persons with little formal education have achieved high vocabulary levels through extensive reading and a constant search for knowledge. But for more rapid vocabulary building and retention of words, the surest way is to learn in the order of difficulty.

Some youngsters more than others need an early start in building vocabulary. The child with strong structural visualization is more interested in things than in ideas; his desire to make things may so overshadow his desire to read and study that extra prodding and help in building vocabulary may be needed. The child with low graphoria also needs an early start. School work is difficult for him; usually he is a slow reader and paperwork is hard for him. An improved vocabulary helps to decrease the difficulty and also builds up the confidence he so often needs. But the child with high graphoria also needs to begin vocabulary building at an early age. School work is easy for him, and he can get by too often without really understanding his studies. Without vocabulary his lack of understanding eventually will cause him to fall behind. These examples are not theories, but facts that are proven in later life.

Although a large, exact vocabulary is of first importance if we want to make the most of our talents and get the most from life, we also need a specialized vocabulary for our particular work. Almost every field has its own jargon which we need to speak to be successful. This is especially crucial in the technical fields. In science and engineering, for example, changes are taking place so rapidly that knowledge in some areas quickly becomes obsolete. Keeping knowledge up-to-date is essential to compete with recent graduates.

Two men recently tested illustrate this point. They had left their jobs in science and engineering, although they had perfect aptitudes for their work, and had gone into jobs completely wrong for their abilities. They had made the change not because they wanted to, but because they felt they could not compete technically with recent college graduates. They admitted they had not kept pace with current knowledge.

Most of us have two vocabularies to acquire—the general and the specific, job-related vocabulary. Books are essential and every effort should be made to build and expand a home library, both general and specialized. Second-hand book stores hold many treasures for little price, and many desirable books are available in paperback. The important thing is to have the books we want readily available so that we can read or refer to them whenever we wish. Individual libraries built around work suited to the highest aptitudes and interests of family members are essential, for this library increases both vocabulary and knowledge in particular fields of interest.

Vocabulary building requires both patience and effort but is well worthwhile. Confucius noted, "Ignorance is the night of the mind, a night without moon or stars." The more we know not only helps to insure greater worldly success, but the knowledge gives us greater inner resources and self-confidence, as well as a deeper understanding of the world we live in.

5

The Executive

Almost any enterprise rewards superior work with executive responsibilities. In business and industry especially, many feel they are unsuccessful unless they have a staff working for them. The promotion to an executive job is the dream of many. The lure of added prestige, more money, and the "sweet smell of success" can be irresistable, and too often a promotion to an executive job is accepted eagerly with little thought of whether it is possible or desirable to direct the work of others.

William James said, "A new position of responsibility will usually show a man to be a far stronger creature than was supposed." This may be true of those promoted only if they have the ability to supervise. The opposite often is true, for a good executive is both born and made. He is born in the sense of possessing certain innate aptitudes, and made in the sense of acquiring knowledge, skill and a character that commands respect.

In more than fifty years of research, testing and follow-up studies, the Laboratory has found that satisfied and effective executives need certain basic attributes: *objective personality, abstract visualization* and *high vocabulary.* This finding may suprise you, for it is contrary to a common belief that the good executive must be gifted with many talents, and be able to do everything his employees can do but do it better. Actually, if he has too many strong aptitudes, he naturally wants to develop them rather than concentrate on developing the abilities of his subordinates. It is difficult for him to delegate authority, to let go of responsibilities that well could be handled by an assistant. Instead of guiding his employees, he may compete with them, often robbing them of initiative and the feeling of responsible accomplishment. While the executive makes policy decisions and carries the load of responsibility, he should do little of the actual work. Rather his job is to get others to do it properly. One prominent executive summed it up: "When problems hit your desk, if you instinctively buck them on to someone else, the chances are strong you're a born boss."

A well-known British admiral was asked how he ever managed to get through the mountains of important work continually piling up in the in-box on his desk. The admiral laughed. "Oh," he replied casually waving at the box, "I just give it a flip onward."

The executive's need for an objective personality is obvious. Because he is outgoing, it is natural for the objective person to be interested in others, to be friendly and accessible, and to try to understand and cope with human frailties and temperaments without becoming emotionally involved. And objectivity helps him handle persons, to inculcate a spirit of teamwork, to be interested and appreciative of the abilities and accomplishments of those beneath him. But there must also be an intangible quality in the executive which commands respect, a quality that stems from a high vocabulary and from the ability to behave without antagonizing others.

The finding that major executives average higher in vocabulary than any other group has been confirmed over the years. The reason is not known, for it would seem that professional people, particularly teachers, editors, lawyers and writers who work with words, would score higher. Perhaps a wide vocabulary indicates not only broad knowledge, but precise knowledge, which an executive must have. He rises or falls on his decisions and certainly knowledge is needed for sound judgment.

One would expect a person would know he was objective and act upon the knowledge. Yet very often the Laboratory tests persons who score definitely objective but are convinced they are subjective and have behaved accordingly. Some years ago, an awkward, shy man was tested. He was so ill-at-ease that the HEL was positive the man must be extremely subjective and low in vocabulary. But the tests showed an objective personality with the traits of the ideal executive. When the HEL told him he should behave like an objective person, the man insisted that this would be putting on a front. Then he thought and said, "Maybe what I've been doing all my life is putting on a front."

Then he asked just why he should behave objectively. He was told that there were two good reasons. "When people behave the way they really are, they are far happier because their behavior agrees with their real personality. You say yourself that you have been very unhappy. Furthermore, you test as an executive, and to get an executive job you must look and act like one. In your present state, no one would hire you for an executive." Established habits are hard to change, but the man did alter his and now holds a high executive position.

On the other hand, objectivity often stands out even if a person who thinks himself subjective and trains for a subjective career then finds himself picked for management. In testing for a large cosmetic company, the human engineers found that the plant manager scored as the ideal executive. This man had begun as a chemist in three different large firms and invariably ended in management. Chemistry requires subjectivity and high structural visualization, but his aptitudes were the exact opposite of those of a chemist. He also scored the highest in vocabulary of the particular group of men being tested. The job of general manager was offered to him. At first he was hesitant about his ability to take such a step forward. But on the basis of his test results, he was persuaded by the vice-president and the human engineers to accept.

The subjective person does not belong in management, for his own sake and for the sake of those he supervises.

His thoughts naturally center on himself, on his own work and not necessarily on the performance of others. He may want to do everything himself, to keep a finger in every pie. Executive work is not natural to him and although he may try hard, he often has difficulty in establishing a real rapport with his subordinates. He is inclined to be inaccessible and see only those persons he wants to see.

An unusual example is the manager of a large grocery supermarket. He is capable and, like most subjectives, very conscientious, but the store chain's personnel manager told the human engineers that the manager has great difficulty in keeping employees. No one can work to please him and his bluntness antagonizes them. He tested to be extremely subjective with low vocabulary. The personnel manager said he was shocked one day when he visited the store to see how haggard the manager looked, so he asked him if anything was wrong or if he was ill. The manager said he was just tired, that he had been working late every night sweeping out the store—no one else could do it well enough to suit him.

Most executives need high abstract visualization. This, you will recall, means a lack of structural visualization ability and an interest in ideas and people. No matter how objective he is, the executive gifted with much structural visualization has a difficult time. The aptitude is basic and demands expression, yet in most executive jobs there is little or no opportunity to use it. Rather the emphasis is on working with people and ideas and he needs an ability to deal in the abstract. Because our unused aptitudes begin to demand the most attention when we reach our late thirties, many executives with high structural visualization resign from the big corporations as they approach forty. In one HEL study, the number was nearly four out of five. The human engineers believe that the person with objective personality and high structural visualization ability, unless he works in architecture, city planning or construction, should start a business in his own field, rather than work for a large corporation.

In our materialistic world, structural visualization

probably is the most salable of all aptitudes. Combined with subjectivity, it characterizes the best engineers, scientists and other technical specialists. Yet the path of promotion invariably points to executive work where these abilities rarely find outlet. As Mr. O'Connor said, "Appointment to an executive desk robs the effective engineer, scientist, and mechanic of the chance of exercising his structural visualization; and though he is honestly happier in structural work, both on the job, at home, and in his mind, he cannot afford to refuse promotion [the way] the business world operates today. To meet this [problem], industry must develop a series of structural titles and salaries equivalent to executive ones."

The human engineers say if you are a good specialist and are offered an executive job, refuse it but insist instead on everything the executive gets—the private office, executive desk and so on. In other words, ask for all the trappings that give prestige to the executive, but stay a specialist and help enhance the image of the specialist in industry.

The working world abounds with subjective persons who have risen to executive posts because they have achieved success in a specialty. They rarely are happy, nor are their subordinates. This is true not only in industry but in many other fields. A college president, for example, might be subjective and enjoy his work until he finds his job involves fund-raising and other group-influencing activities. Government has its share of subjective executives because of the merit system of promotion and the incorporation of executive responsibilities at higher grade levels.

An unfortunate case is that of an attractive, middle-aged man with many years of government service who supervises as many as thirty highly-trained professionals. When tested, he proved to be extremely subjective with high structural visualization and ideaphoria. His work is completely non-structural, but creative, and for his own sake and for the sake of his staff he should have stayed in the scientific work for which he trained in college. At work he vents his frustrations in a volatile temper and a cold and sarcastic treatment of his staff. He admits he knows the staff hates him, but that his work gets on his nerves so much he can't control himself. His real interests center in sculpture and anthropology, and when he talks of these he seems a different person. But he feels at his age he can't afford to change jobs. He has developed ulcers and looks forward only to retiring.

This individual not only has high structural visualization and subjectivity working against him in an executive job, but he has strong ideaphoria. Most executives are better off with little or none of this trait which gives its possessor a rapid flow of ideas. The exceptions are sales and merchandising executives and perhaps those in advertising and public relations. The executive with high ideaphoria is bored by routine and details and always wants to stir up some action. He no sooner gets something started than he must try something different, while his subordinates barely have adjusted to his last fancy. Often they are left confused and pressured, robbed of the satisfaction of completing a job well before proceeding to the next.

The best trait of a teacher is ideaphoria. Yet school officials often take the best teachers and reward them with administrative jobs. The human engineers test many teachers who have perfect aptitudes for teaching but want to quit and get into other work. A common reason given is that they have difficulty working under their supervisors.

High ideaphoria can play hob with an executive unless he has an outlet for it. One man with the executive aptitude pattern but with high ideaphoria was made general manager of a manufacturing plant. He was so bored and restless he developed stomach trouble and a variety of nervous disorders. He was moved into sales and almost at once his physical problems disappeared—high ideaphoria is the primary trait of salesmen. Although the executive is better off without ideaphoria, he needs highly creative persons working under him; without them he would have a dull organization. His job is to evaluate and use the best ideas of his subordinates.

High ideaphoria needs another aptitude to guide it, and often the one most needed is inductive reasoning. Most executives, particularly in the big corporations, have low inductive reasoning, but top officials in merchandising and sales planning are high in this trait. Perhaps an important reason most executives have little of this aptitude is that the highly inductive person has difficulty reaching a decision. His ability to put scattered facts together quickly puts too many angles and ideas in his way and he has trouble making up his mind. In a new situation, the highly inductive person comes out more often with the right answer, but he dislikes making a decision and puts it off, arguing with himself and wanting more facts. The person with low inductive ability may be wrong, but at least he makes a decision and goes on from there. He relies heavily on experience and high vocabulary. When we consider that most major decisions in business and industry involve long and costly procedures, the reason for low inductive reasoning becomes quite clear. Time is needed to think things through, to weigh matters carefully before making a final decision and taking action.

High inductive reasoning is a characteristic of many successful government executives, and may be the reason why so many in top posts have law backgrounds. This aptitude is the primary trait of lawyers. One top government executive who has low inductive reasoning says he uses his high vocabulary to compensate for the deficiency. In high-level meetings, he says he sits back and listens to the high-inductive people talking and arguing. Then, with time and high vocabulary in his favor, and the reluctance of the others to make a decision, he proposes a solution often accepted by the group. He has developed a reputation for sound judgment.

Low inductive reasoning ability in most executives may explain why they have the highest vocabulary. If we have much of this aptitude we are inclined to guess at word meanings, to jump at conclusions. The person low in the aptitude must look things up and dig out the facts for himself, and consequently may gain more exact knowledge. And also, because the born executive has few high aptitudes, over the years he may have lacked much interest in hobbies, and been pushed into reading as a diversion.

At one time, the Laboratory said that the executive should have high graphoria. The human engineers no longer believe this to be true, except for bankers and others who deal primarily with figures and paperwork. A good executive has a staff to handle the paperwork. And it may be that if the executive is very strong in graphoria, he would want to spend too much time on details, neglecting more important executive responsibilities.

If we have the basic executive traits and other strong aptitudes, the human engineers believe we would get the most satisfaction from doing administrative work in the field of these aptitudes, and would have far more opportunity to be ourselves and find self-expression. For example, with strong music aptitudes, we would be happiest in executive work in some aspect of sound or music. Several years ago a young real estate broker came to take the Laboratory's worksamples. He said he disliked his work intensely, and was getting so depressed he could stand it no longer. He had the executive pattern and very high music aptitudes. These results interested him greatly as all his life music and dancing had meant much to him. Though he had served a short stint as a ballroom dance instructor, he never had considered music a real career. When dance management was suggested, it sparked his imagination. His home is located in a well-known art and music center, and he felt that in such a place there must be somewhere he could use his music. He sold his business and enrolled in a dance school. In little more than a year, he had absorbed many dancing techniques and principles of choreography and ballet. Choreography interested him most of all and he is now on the production management staff of a prominent ballet group.

There is a great need for real executives. Perhaps the greatest complaint made by workers is directed at their supervisors. Most of us would agree that a good boss, like the good woman in the Proverbs, "has a price above rubies." To be a good and successful executive, we most need the ability to get along well with others and to acquire a broad and exact knowledge, not only of our work, but of people and the world.

36

6.

The Lawyer

In our troubled times, the importance of law and order stands out sharply. Lawlessness is a synonym for terror and chaos, a destructive force that erodes the quality of life and threatens the survival of civilization. Law touches the lives of all of us; it is the means by which a government maintains stability and establishes justice for its citizens, giving maximum freedom to the individual without denying such freedom to others. It is easy to see why law is one of the most respected of the professions.

Whether on the bench or in private practice, a lawyer must analyze and utilize the law in cases involving every kind of person and situation. For this he needs both extensive legal and broad general knowledge. Fortunately, the study of law is so comprehensive and exacting it almost always results in a high vocabulary. Thomas Jefferson advised the law student to make all knowledge his province, that legal knowledge was not enough. When Justice Holmes was a student at Harvard Law School he described the study of law as "a mind trainer." And certainly law, like all of the learned professions, must be approached through a mass of dry technicalities.

The ideal aptitudes for a lawyer are subjective personality, high inductive reasoning and abstract visualization with a high vocabulary. Statistically, this pattern occurs in one man out of two hundred and fifty-six and more often in women. The human engineers advise young persons who have only these aptitudes and no others, except perhaps graphoria which is useful anywhere, to investigate law as a career.

Of all aptitudes, inductive reasoning is of first importance to a lawyer. If we have high inductive reasoning we can take apparently unrelated facts or ideas and detect the common thread that joins them into a pattern. We see things quickly; with low inductive reasoning you might say it almost takes a blueprint to make us see it. A lawyer must be able to take scattered facts, bits of evidence and principles of law and correlate them. In preparing for court, for example, he must investigate facts and the evidence his client gives him, interview witnesses, review documents, and prepare and file pleadings in court. Also, the high-inductive person likes to argue. In a court trial, his arguments are subject to constant attack and must be well reasoned. These are all reasons why he also needs a high vocabulary.

Strong inductive reasoning without vocabulary can be a dangerous thing. Mr. O'Connor told the story of an eighteen-year-old reform school youth who scored 100 per cent in inductive reasoning and at the very bottom in vocabulary. He asked the young man, "How can you stand knowing you are right, with 100 per cent inductive and no words to convince others?" The young man shook his fist. "I do it this way. That's why I'm back in the reformatory for the third time." Too often strong inductive reasoning coupled with low vocabulary spells violence. Without words for argument and reason, the fists do the arguing.

You cannot be a successful lawyer without inductive reasoning, nor can you be content in the profession. One lawyer who tested low in inductive reasoning dislikes his work so intensely and feels so unsure of himself in it, despite a high vocabulary, that he has become an alcoholic. And more women than men have inductive reasoning. Perhaps what we think of as feminine intuition isn't so much pure hunch as it is possession of this trait. Portia was not a trained lawyer and if you wonder how she handled Shylock's case with such rare intuition at such a young age, some explanation may be found in the fact that the aptitude of inductive reasoning is fully mature at the age of eighteen.

Those persons who have inductive reasoning as their strongest aptitude are the ones most inclined to seek reforms, to be dissenters. Without vocabulary, this dissent may find expression in violence and futile protestations; with high vocabulary it can mean positive reform for human good. In his day, Holmes was known as "The Great Dissenter," but it was not the number but the quality of his dissents that made them famous, a quality that stemmed from his wide knowledge.

Subjective personality is important to a lawyer, partly because of the long hours of isolated study involved but also because, like the doctor, he works with the individual client rather than with groups of people. In law practice, each case is under the lawyer's own control. Also, the subjective person is inclined to take up causes, to fight for what he believes regardless of what others think. Many young persons go into law with the dreams of charting new courses in law, of bringing about reforms in jurisprudence. Those who do this, in the words of Holmes, "must face the loneliness of original work. No one can cut new paths in company. He does it alone."

But there is yet another reason why a lawyer needs to be subjective. Because of his outgoing nature, the objective lawyer may be too anxious to please others. But the profession itself is extremely subjective, and the code of ethics so high that anyone who violates it may find himself in severe trouble.

The objective person who has disciplined himself to acquire a legal background has a valuable asset, although probably he should not use his training in private practice but in more objective ways. There are many opportunities for him in the legal aspects of business. Or he might go into politics, diplomacy, or any work of similar nature where a knowledge of law and the ability to work with others is desirable. Government is based on law and many whose political life has led to high government posts or Congress have this combination of legal background and objectivity. But the ones who are the true leaders usually are subjective, playing their role much as an actor would do, but with the zeal and crusading spirit found so often in subjective persons.

However, politicians need high ideaphoria, and if there is one place this trait does not belong it is in law practice. Certainly a judge needs to be low in creative imagination to exercise sound judgment. In general, lawyers do not need ideaphoria—with the exception of perhaps the trial lawyers who must defend a case in court. Highly creative persons get restless and bored and often leave law practice to enter politics or seek other outlets. In the past few years, the Laboratory has tested at least seven high-vocabulary lawyers with legal aptitudes, but with high ideaphoria, who are so dissatisfied in law practice that they have groped in various ways to find expression for the trait. One has left law several times and currently is selling stocks and bonds; another runs a radio program four nights a week; a third is executive secretary of a political committee, and so on.

Some lawyers with high ideaphoria write novels, for the legal aptitudes coupled with it characterize successful creative writers. Actually, some very well-known authors have started out to be lawyers. Galsworthy, for example, was admitted to the bar but practiced little, yet his knowledge of law served him well in creating *The Forsyte Saga.* Even Thackeray, as you may recall, left law to write, and the influence of his legal training perhaps is most apparent in *Pendennis.*

While the subjective young person with legal aptitudes combined with ideaphoria might go into law as an approach to a future political career, there are pitfalls here. It is true that occasionally a man at the top in politics is subjective. But because he is subjective he must start at the top, and with high ideaphoria few lawyers rise high enough in their profession to move easily from law practice to the top in politics. Another reason often given for getting a law background as an approach to politics is that you always have a secure profession to go back to, but the high-ideaphoria person is not happy in law practice and rarely becomes successful in it.

There always are exceptions, but from long research and testing the human engineers are quite convinced that college teaching or editorial writing, which use the same aptitudes, are better approaches for the subjective, high-ideaphoria person than is law. On the other hand, the older person who already has a law degree, but whose high ideaphoria makes him restless in the confines of law practice, often finds politics or diplomacy a desirable answer to his problem. Many of our Presidents have had a law background —both Adamses, Jefferson, Lincoln, both Roosevelts, you can name a great many more. The only President measured by the Laboratory tested subjective with high ideaphoria and inductive reasoning and low structural visualization. His educational background, however, was not in law.

Because law deals in abstract concepts, most lawyers need to be low in structural visualization and thus high in abstract visualization. As a rule, persons strong in structural thinking do not belong in law. An exception might be patent lawyers who must often understand technical drawings and diagrams. Or a person with structural ability and legal training might fit into the legal aspects of such structural fields as building construction and city planning. Also, extreme subjectivity, high structural visualization and inductive reasoning are the aptitudes of the problem-solver. Outstanding advances have been made by applying the techniques of one field of knowledge to another, such as biochemistry, astrophysics and the like. An intriguing problem might be that of combining science with law and applying scientific procedures to the solution of legal problems.

To most lawyers, graphoria is not essential, but its lack makes completing law school harder. Lawyers who greatly need this accounting aptitude are tax and estate lawyers whose work involves much dealing with figures. Foresight may be important to a lawyer in order to stick to the goal of becoming a lawyer and, later, to pursue his ultimate objectives. The low-foresight person sees only the immediate goal and often needs outside encouragement to stay with a long-range plan.

One low-foresight college student, who had ideal legal aptitudes and had planned to become a lawyer, took a summer job as a waiter in a fashionable resort hotel. The tips were generous and the atmosphere pleasant. Making good money, he decided to quit school. He worked for some years as a waiter, but later regretted not having completed law school as he was too old to start again.

Because inductive reasoning is the aptitude of the professions, the human engineers urge anyone who tests subjective and strong in the trait to continue formal education as long as possible. They have seen too many tragic cases of high-inductive subjectives with no training upon which to build a satisfactory life work. Almost every job using high inductive reasoning requires a background of higher education and often graduate work—law, medicine, science, teaching, and so on. And any subjective person needs a specialty in keeping with his strongest aptitudes if he is to get satisfaction in life, or even get any kind of a decent job.

Ironically, the subjective person often creates his own defeat. He may concentrate all his efforts on building up his weakest traits, sometimes because this represents to him the most in hard work and suffering, or he may avoid using his strongest abilities for fear of never reaching an ideal he has set for himself. Too often the result is a mental breakdown. The Laboratory is convinced that at least half if not more of the mental cases in hospitals today are subjectives who never found their niche in life.

In making a career in law, or in any work, much depends on your goal in life, whether it is to make money, gain prestige or power, be of service, or make the world a better place. There was one young law student who long had cherished a dream of working eventually in a large Chicago law firm. It was the one firm in the entire country that he had set his heart on and, by a stroke of luck, he secured a summer job there at an unusually high salary. But when he came back to school he announced that this was not for him, nor was any large law office. When asked why, he replied, "I was only an employee." He had grown up in the slums, and his plans now are to go back to his own people to practice law, to do what he can to help them with their legal problems.

Prodded by a deep desire to become a lawyer, this young man, who has ideal law aptitudes and a high vocabulary, has worked hard to put himself through school, working summers and after hours to get the money. There are many others who, despite financial obstacles, have managed through hard work and sheer determination to do it.

A heartening story is that of a woman lawyer who did it the hard way and now has her own thriving law firm. At the time she graduated from high school, her parents had suffered financial reverses and could not afford to send her to college. She took a business course and went to work as a typist. For some years she did this, and other office work of a more responsible nature, but felt she was getting nowhere. As she says, "I wanted to get going, to make more of myself." She was well into her thirties when she decided to go to night law school. It was not easy to work all day and attend school and study at night, but she eventually graduated from law school, took her examinations and was admitted to the bar. She loves her work and never has regretted that she had the courage and determination to study law, and certainly her experience has made her all the more sympathetic and understanding in dealing with her clients and their problems.

Although the lawyer needs a high vocabulary to rise in his profession, there is another matter of great importance to him when he enters practice where vocabulary plays a part. This is passing state bar examinations. Varying in different states, some are so rigid that a high vocabulary is essential to pass them. The Laboratory once tested a man who scored as the ideal lawyer but had failed twice to pass his bar examinations. At the time, he was certain he never would be admitted to the bar and took the HEL tests to discover what else he might do. He wanted to practice more than anything else but was so discouraged about failing the examinations that he thought it was hopeless and was about to give it up.

His vocabulary level was below bar admittance standards in the state where he was trying. It was suggested that he study the requirements of various states, select one that exacted the least, and try to pass the examination there. He did this, passed and was admitted to the bar and began his practice in that state. But he wanted to settle permanently in the state where he had first tried so he decided to follow the Laboratory's advice and build vocabulary. After three years, he went back and tried the examinations there again. This time he passed.

A lawyer must have not only wide and exact knowledge, but must be able to express himself fluently. Some years ago, a fifty-seven year old lawyer was tested and proved to have perfect aptitudes for law and a high vocabulary. Despite ability and great charm, he was only moderately successful. His trouble was that he stammered badly. The tests had showed him to be left-eyed and right-handed, and it was pointed out to him that the tension induced by this crossed dominance could well cause the stammering. He was told that if he would try very gradually to make himself left-handed he might be able to cure his handicap. He did nothing about it until he had retired at sixty from law practice. Then he began the process of making himself use his left hand, starting with simple actions, for the changeover must be gradual or the nervous strain is exaggerated. Three years later he came back to the Laboratory, amazed to report that he no longer stammered. He said he would give anything if he had known this years ago, for he knew that his law career had been hampered by his inability to be a forceful and persuasive speaker.

Man's social development is the history of law. The challenge to lawyers today is great. With changing times and changing needs, law itself must change with the times, and lawyers have a vital role in bringing jurisprudence to greater heights. Gifted as they are with inductive reasoning, they can be the diagnosticians of many of the world's social ills.

7

The Engineer

A good half of the world's work today demands structural thinking in which engineers play an important role. The incredible achievements in engineering and their impact on our way of life make it difficult to realize that the profession once was confined to the military and its emergence into civilian life slow and gradual, with training acquired by apprenticeship. The first known formal education for engineers began in France in 1747. In mid-nineteenth century, there were only six colleges in the United States that granted degrees in engineering. A hundred years later, there were more than one hundred and fifty.

With the growth of engineering has come the need for more specialized technical and scientific knowledge. No longer can a man or woman go into general engineering and expect to achieve much success. Specialization encompasses so many areas that almost any aptitude pattern can be fitted to engineering, provided the pattern includes high structural visualization. This is the all-important aptitude, for without it you can't be a true engineer.

Most engineers are subjective, but some are objective. And depending on the type of engineering, the aptitude patterns are divergent. For example, a construction engineer is objective with low ideaphoria, while a design engineer is the opposite with subjectivity and high creativity. The engineering in which we specialize should be compatible with our strongest aptitudes if we are to give it our best efforts and derive the most satisfaction from it. For example, sound engineering utilizes musical aptitudes; design engineering uses memory for design; cost engineering needs graphoria, and so on.

Why structural visualization is the primary aptitude is obvious. The engineer must be able to visualize solids; certainly he must have the aptitude to read a blueprint.

Several years ago, one of the most disheveled and despondent looking young men the Laboratory has ever encountered came in for the tests. He needed a shave; his clothes looked as if he had slept in them; his eyes were bloodshot; and his whole appearance that of a person who had reached the end of his rope. At first the test administrator thought perhaps he had been drinking or using drugs but soon learned that this was not true.

In the process of taking the worksamples and later in evaluating the summary, his story came out. After receiving his degree in civil engineering he had been inducted into the Army. Completing officer's training, he was assigned first to telephone installation and then to repairing and maintaining aircraft armament, followed by nine months of Army aircraft maintenance. Now back in civilian life, he had taken a job with a State Department of Highways and assigned to bridge construction. His major assignment and the one that, as he said, "really put the tin hat on it," was to compute from blueprints how much concrete would be needed to build a certain bridge unit.

It was his first important assignment and he was eager to do a good job. He said he had pored over the blueprints for days and some nights. "The blueprints showed the bridge at an angle," he said. "The outlines of the bridge didn't face me squarely and I just couldn't *see* it." After a hard struggle, he had mailed his report to the State office for approval. It had been returned to him with red marks on both margins and texts, interspersed with sarcastic and humiliating remarks and questions. He said he felt as if he never could hold up his head again. He had worked so hard, had given the best he knew how to give, and had failed miserably.

If it is possible to be totally lacking in an aptitude, this man was totally lacking in structural visualization. Yet ever since college he had been trying to function either as a mechanical specialist or engineer. One can only hope that while in the service someone checked his work. His relief at knowing that this lack of structural visualization was the cause of his downfall was intense, and he became eager to plan what he could do that would be in keeping with his aptitudes and interests. In addition to low structure visualization, he proved to be extremely subjective with high tweezer dexterity, observation and graphoria and low vocabulary.

He said agriculture always had interested him, that he had grown up on a farm and loved to work outdoors. He managed to transfer to the Department of Agriculture where he is working on an experimental project. His job includes caring for plants and trees; preparing, mounting and examining microscope slides, which uses both tweezer dexterity and observation; and writing progress reports. Meanwhile he is working to raise his vocabulary to improve his fitness for writing and increase his chance for advancement in his new field. The important thing is that he likes his work and says he is happy to be out of engineering. He had gone into engineering because of the opportunities in the field, misled by his ability to work with his hands, but he said his heart never had been in his profession.

Another young engineer unenthusiastic about his work tested objective with low structural visualization and at the very top in inductive reasoning. He was far more interested in establishing a labor union than in his engineering work. While scientists have high inductive reasoning, engineers average low in the trait. The lack of structural visualization of course would account for this young man's indifference to engineering, but the persons who have inductive reasoning as their strongest aptitude are the most inclined to take up causes. They sense things wrong more quickly than others and tend to criticize. If low vocabulary, they can be prime troublemakers, but if high vocabulary they can help to bring about important changes and improvements.

Most engineers and mechanics have the aptitude for

proportion appraisal. The human engineers are not certain of the reason. This ability to discern pleasing proportions once was believed to be an art aptitude but artists and architects score low in it. It may be that the test measures a feeling for doing things in a methodical way, following rules and precedents and a rigid discipline. The low-scoring person likes to work out a new way of attacking each problem, unhampered by previous conceptions.

Although most of us think of the music aptitudes mainly in terms of playing an instrument or singing, they are useful in any kind of engineering where mechanical equipment is used. They enable the engineer to note changes in the sound of a motor, or changes in any operation that creates a noise.

Most engineers are subjective but some such as civil and chemical engineers often are objective. The main problem with the objective personality-structural visualization combination is that your outgoing nature draws you to work with people and your structural visualization pulls you to work with things. When objective engineers can combine administrative duties with structural work, they experience few difficulties. But, as mentioned earlier, too often in the large corporations when engineers rise to executive rank they have little chance to use their structural visualization. The Laboratory recommends that the high-structure executive should not behave as the high abstract one does, who sits at his desk and directs, but should get out into the factory or into the research laboratory for at least part of his time.

From past research, the human engineers know that unused structural visualization generates restlessness and dissatisfaction with self and accomplishments that affects work, family relations, and the whole of life. This, perhaps, is why so many high-structure executives resign from the big corporations at a time in life when they have achieved enviable success in the eyes of the world, but not in their own estimation.

Recently I talked with an engineer who had just resigned from a top executive job in a very large corporation.

Taking the Laboratory's worksamples when he was in college, he had scored objective with high structural visualization, memory for design and tonal memory, average ideaphoria and low inductive reasoning. Although he had started as an engineer, as he acquired experience he invariably was promoted to managerial positions which he enjoyed so long as he could use his structural visualization. But the higher he went, the less chance he had to use it. He said all his work was with people, he wasn't happy and so he resigned. He has joined a small technical company as an executive working with many outside scientists and engineers, planning future needs and solving technical problems. He says he enjoys the work and thinks he has solved his problem of combining objectivity with structural visualization.

Another man, a mechanical engineer, started his career as a project engineer. Subsequent jobs involved the supervision of others and at present he is chief engineer for a missile project. He says he enjoys organization, planning and management work, but that he also uses his structural visualization every day on the job. He was surprised to learn he was objective, for he tends to be shy and reserved and had always thought himself to be subjective, and, as he said, never had been overly outgoing in his behavior. This does not mean to imply that objective persons necessarily are very outgoing. The truth is that among high vocabulary persons it often is difficult to distinguish between objective and subjective personality by behavior. Usually it is only among the very low vocabulary persons that you find the boisterous back-slapper and shrinking violet types.

As you may recall, the usual engineer aptitude pattern of structural visualization and subjective personality runs counter to the successful executive one of objectivity and high abstract visualization. Yet, as pointed out previously, the management of many industries selects men for exclusively executive work from among their most capable engineers, and in so doing loses superior engineers to gain only inferior and unhappy executives.

Some years ago, a sound engineer was tested in Chicago. He had been employed for ten years by one of the largest companies in the sound and communications field, and was considered one of its finest engineers. He had ideal aptitudes for his work—subjectivity, structural visualization, the music aptitudes and tweezer dexterity—but was below average in vocabulary. His work had been so outstanding that the management thought he should be rewarded, and so took him out of engineering and placed him in a high executive position. At first he was thrilled, for it meant prestige, recognition and more money.

However, he was such a failure as an executive that he was soon put back in his old engineering job. What this reverse has done to him personally is tragic. He feels that going back to his old job was a demotion and that he has failed completely in life. He has lost interest in everything, drinks heavily, neglects his work and his family, and is so dispirited that he has encased himself in a shell which no one can penetrate. He cannot understand that the born executive and the born engineer are opposites, or that success in one type of work doesn't guarantee success in another. He is convinced that life has no more to offer him. He lacks the vocabulary to see what is the matter and to rise above his problem.

Although there are many engineers who have high vocabulary, in general they have only an average one. This vocabulary level can be attributed to high structural visualization which often interferes with a youngster's ability to build vocabulary. The child naturally is drawn to things rather than ideas, and prefers building models or tinkering with machines to reading and study. The same is true of girls who have high structural visualization, except they choose more feminine activities. Such children usually need to be stimulated to build vocabulary.

Another deterrent to vocabulary building can be a natural disinterest in abstract ideas. One engineer said he never had much appreciation for philosophy or any abstract ideas. "When I was in college," he said, "I was required to take a course in the philosophy of science and to this day I have no idea what the instructor was trying to teach me, although I put in a lot of time on the course."

Engineers need vocabulary. If we have aptitudes we

must have the vocabulary to go with them. Mechanics, machinists, draftsmen and engineers all have the same aptitudes; the difference lies in vocabulary level. One cannot do engineering with a mechanic's vocabulary. Recently the Laboratory tested an engineer from Europe who had immigrated to the United States. He said he was getting nowhere in his work. He proved to have every aptitude for engineering but he scored at the very bottom in English vocabulary. His native language vocabulary level may have been very high, but to succeed in this country, he needs an English vocabulary on a level with other engineers.

For greatest success and satisfaction, engineers need both a wide general and a strong technical vocabulary. The human engineers have found that there is a close relationship between a physics vocabulary and a general one, and that it is almost impossible to acquire a technical vocabulary without a general vocabulary to back it up. In one study, only seven of 858 persons scored high in the physics vocabulary test and low in the general. Two of these men, although strong in technical knowledge, have mediocre engineering jobs and never seem to get any further ahead. This, of course, is in keeping with the Laboratory's finding that the most successful are those with high vocabulary.

In these times of rapid technological change, it is imperative for the engineer to keep abreast of his profession. Successful engineers say that they must read technical journals and new books in their fields with unrelenting regularity, for changes are so rapid that otherwise their knowledge would soon become obsolete. It is also imperative for the engineer, or one who aspires to be one, to build broad general knowledge, for the sake of his own advancement and for applying his talent and skills where they will do the most good. These are thrilling times for the born engineer, not only in helping to solve earthly problems, but in adding to our knowledge of space and of the ocean depths. The aptitude of structural visualization is far more than mechanical ability. It is a problem-solving gift, and the born engineer who lifts his sights and increases his knowledge is well-equipped to help solve many of the problems that face the world today.

8

Medicine and Health

The serpents on the caduceus bring to mind that people in some parts of the world once believed in the healing powers of snakes, or placed their faith in other superstitions to make them well. Over the centuries men have made significant contributions to medical knowledge, but it was only a little over a hundred years ago that men such as Pasteur and Lister laid the foundations for medical science as we know it today.

As incredible as it may seem, as recently as fifty years ago the only drugs found in a doctor's satchel, apart from usual analgesics, antitoxins, and anesthetics, were quinine, opium, digitalis, mercury and iodine. The upsurge of medical knowledge that began in the 1930's has been growing in momentum ever since. The field is so varied that there is a place for almost anyone who wants to alleviate physical and mental suffering and to be a part in the conquest of illness, disease and abnormalities.

We may never see the researchers and other technicians behind the scenes, but most of us do see doctors, perhaps most frequently general practitioners, diagnosticians and dentists. So far as aptitudes are concerned, the "family doctor" needs inductive reasoning more than any other trait. He must be able to diagnose us so he can determine proper treatment. To keep from going off on feckless tangents in his diagnoses, he needs to be low in ideaphoria. Tweezer dexterity is desirable for easy handling of medical instruments and, because long and irregular hours demand great physical energy, it might be well for him to score high in grip, the experimental worksample that seems indicative of physical strength and endurance.

Structural visualization is not so essential to the diagnostician as it is to the surgeon, but it is helpful in getting through medical school, particularly in anatomy courses. One of the leading U.S. diagnosticians lacks structural visualization; furthermore he says he had great difficulty with his anatomy studies in school. And it took two young men both low in structural visualization three years to struggle through anatomy, but both are now successful doctors, one a diagnostician, the other a psychiatrist.

As a rule, doctors need to be subjective, first to pursue their studies with the intensity needed to gain such vast specialized knowledge and later, in private practice, to be content working with the individual patient. They also need pitch discrimination which shows keenness of perception.

Surgeons and dentists need both subjectivity and high inductive reasoning but, above all, they must have high structural visualization and tweezer dexterity. The reasons are obvious. When an incision is made in our own flesh we want the surgeon to know precisely where and how deep to cut and to handle his instruments with a sure hand. We want our dentist to know exactly how deep to drill or how to poke and pry without fumbling. And structural visualization also is essential to him in constructing proper-fitting inlays and dentures, and in really understanding dental structure.

The importance of tweezer dexterity to a surgeon should not be underestimated. It can mean the difference between a successful and an unsuccessful operation. This ability to handle small instruments deftly and precisely is all-important when every second counts and the least bit of clumsiness can spell disaster. The successful surgeon also needs analytical reasoning and low ideaphoria: he must see the answer to complex anatomical problems almost instinctively and must not be diverted in his reasoning.

When human life is at stake, the necessity for the right aptitudes, skill and knowledge looms large. Often the doctor, and especially the surgeon, must rely on instincts in an emergency when there is no time to depend on reasoning and acquired skill. With the necessary aptitudes he can work well under pressure.

As a whole, the medical profession except public health officials and medical teachers, averages low ideaphoria. Quite often the Laboratory tests young men and women whose aptitudes show that they do not belong in medicine, but who are convinced that this is where they want to be. High ideaphoria often leads them to imagine the glamour of the profession without picturing the restrictive daily life many doctors must lead. With some there are visions of community prestige and contributions to humanity. Then, after spending some time in medical school they decide their motivation is not strong enough to devote their lives to medicine. Often their interest lies in something medicine offers which they can find elsewhere, perhaps in religion, teaching, or some social service work where they can feel they are helping humanity and for which their aptitudes are better suited.

One young man, a high school junior, was determined to enter medicine. The tests, however, showed him to be objective with very strong ideaphoria, structural visualization, inductive reasoning and memory for design. When it was explained to him that architecture would be far more suited to his aptitudes than medicine, that in ordinary medicine his objectivity and ideaphoria would create problems, he insisted he still wanted a career in medicine. His real interests were there, and true interests are too precious to be thwarted. When it was suggested that he study architecture with the objective of designing medical structures, that he could help humanity, for example, by creating a hospital that combined environmental beauty with utility, he became enthusiastic about the idea. He is now heading in that direction.

The Laboratory has found that many students wanting a medical career are afraid to take the aptitude tests for fear of discovering an unfitness for the profession. Why this reaction should be true of medicine more than other fields is a puzzle. One reason may be the rare opportunity of a son to take over his father's established practice. And statistically, sons who follow fathers succeed as a group, for at home they pick up the vocabulary of the profession. One fourteen-year-old son of a doctor scored 96 per cent correct in the Laboratory's medical vocabulary test, higher than many practicing physicians. The Laboratory believes that if anyone wants medicine seriously enough to persist with it, they should do so but make necessary adjustments based on aptitudes.

One young doctor had practiced medicine for two years and disliked it so intensely that he came for testing to find out what else he might do. He said that he had worked hard to fulfill the dreams of becoming a doctor, but now his work was becoming a nightmare to him. He scored low in both structural visualization and inductive reasoning and very high in all the music aptitudes, ideaphoria, and both general and music vocabulary. Where to fit in medicine was a problem, for even with low structural visualization he lacked the inductive reasoning needed for diagnostic medicine or psychiatry. But his unhappiness stemmed not only from the inaptitude for his work, but from his idle music aptitudes and his repressed ideaphoria.

His years of medical study should not be wasted, nor should his knowledge of music. It was suggested that he might try to combine the two, perhaps in the therapeutic effects of music. Another possibility might be medical photography of some kind, because photographers seem to score high in both tonal memory and pitch discrimination. The interpretation of x-rays, however, requires structural visualization.

Sometimes a single aptitude can spoil a medical career. One young man, who all his life had planned to become a surgeon like his outstanding surgeon father, started medical school and did well until he began work in surgical procedures. Then he panicked and said he could not continue. The father thought his aversion was plain cowardice and stubbornness, and there was so much quarreling at home about it that life was becoming unbearable for the whole family. The young man said he couldn't explain it; he only knew he could not go on with surgery.

A family friend who knew of the tense situation suggested that the young man be tested by the Laboratory, that an outside opinion might be helpful. The father was skeptical, but agreed grudgingly.

The young man proved to be subjective with extremely high structural visualization and the other aptitudes ideal for a surgeon—except for one thing. He had no tweezer dexterity whatsoever. It is easy to see how this lack could make him instinctively unsure of himself in work that requires the utmost adroitness in handling small instruments. Although surgery could utilize his very high structural visualization, tweezer dexterity would be essential. He had ideal aptitudes for engineering and, after even more emotional conflict at home, he changed to engineering school and has since become an outstanding engineer.

Doctors in private practice need to be subjective to enjoy their work with individual patients. But with the shortage of doctors today, most of them are kept so busy they have no time for research. Yet they need to conduct research not only to become more knowledgeable in a specialty but to give their subjectivity fuller outlet. After seeing patients all day long, doctors need to get off by themselves and work alone. The human engineers advise young doctors to put aside a day each week for research to get the most satisfaction from their work.

Although group medicine is giving the more objective doctors a chance to exercise their outgoing natures, the fact remains that objectivity can create problems, particularly for a surgeon. In almost any work it is difficult to combine objective personality with high structural visualization, but in surgery it is even more so. Some years ago, four successful surgeons who were tested by the Laboratory complained that despite their success they were unaccountably bored and restless. All had strong structural visualization, tweezer dexterity and high general and medical vocabularies, and all were objective. All saw in objectivity a reason for their distress and each set about to adjust his work.

One became the dean of a medical school but still did not feel this was the answer; another became a medical school administrator but remained dissatisfied; the third became manager of a large hospital and still was restless. The fourth turned to teaching part-time in a medical school, devoting the rest of the time to private practice. He feels he has come the closest to solving his problem of combining surgery with objective personality. The others found they missed the surgical problems and, while they were using their objectivity, their structural visualization and tweezer dexterity were not being used.

Objective doctors are inclined to become restive in private practice. Some solve their problem by dividing their time between private practice and work at a public clinic. One distinguished diagnostician not only was restless in private practice, but was deeply dissatisfied with himself. He told the human engineers he had entered medicine with profound ideals of serving humanity, of giving of himself to help anyone who needed him. His office was in a wealthy, fashionable neighborhood and he had a large and lucrative practice. His clients were well-fed and well-cared for and could afford the services of any specialist they might choose. No poor and needy person ever came to him and he felt he was not giving his services where they were most needed.

He tested objective with all the other aptitudes of a diagnostician and with a very high vocabulary. When it was pointed out that his objectivity was contributing to his restlessness and that he could find an outlet in operating a public clinic, he decided to open one in a slum area. He spends half of his time at the clinic and the other half in his private practice, and reports that he gets great satisfaction from it, that to him it answers his desires and needs.

Objective dentists who become dissatisfied with private practice often find an answer in part-time teaching or clinic work. But when a dentist also has high ideaphoria he not only can become bored with routine work, but can encounter unexpected difficulties. One such dentist was almost ready to forsake his career and go into sales or advertising when he was tested. He proved to have the necessary structural visualization and tweezer dexterity, but was convinced he was not a good dentist because he simply could not perfect his techniques. Other dentists could, he said, so something must be wrong with him.

In discussing his problem, the cause gradually came to light. He had no outlet for his high creativity in his dental work except for rearranging his office and equipment almost daily. He bought every new gadget that came on the market and was constantly trying them out. Each day everything would be in a different place, different instruments would be used, and it is small wonder he could not develop techniques. To perfect a procedure it must be repeated over and over in the same way. When he was told he was behaving like a creative housewife who, when she has no other outlet for ideaphoria, keeps changing the furniture around, he laughed and said he saw the picture perfectly. To give an outlet for both objectivity and ideaphoria, he opened a public clinic part-time in conjunction with his private practice and expresses his ideaphoria in developing and promoting new ideas for the clinic. And he says his techniques have improved since he stopped moving the furniture.

Some doctors find an outlet for high ideaphoria in writing. A. J. Cronin, for example, must have had high ideaphoria to create his magnificent novels. Although most doctors are more content in their work if they lack the aptitude, psychiatrists need to be strong in that trait. They need also both inductive and analytical reasoning, subjectivity, abstract visualization and a high general and medical vocabulary.

Occupational therapy seems to be a field especially suited to women. In general, the occupational therapist needs ideaphoria, structural visualization and finger or tweezer dexterity. Perhaps either personality can be suitable, but objectivity may be the more desirable since many patients to whom such therapy is given are consumed with emotional problems, and the objective person often is better equipped to cope with them than is the subjective.

The nursing profession always has attracted women,

and certainly the demand for trained nurses is greater now than ever. Because she carries on where the doctor leaves off, her job requires both competence and understanding. For this reason, and for good doctor and patient relations she needs a fairly high vocabulary. One Laboratory study of student nurses found that those with low vocabulary never complete nurses' training, and those with very high scores leave the profession.

By way of aptitudes, a nurse needs high graphoria and tweezer dexterity, and low ideaphoria. She may, or may not have structural visualization. Of all the traits, graphoria is perhaps the most necessary of all. She cannot afford to make mistakes in carrying out the doctor's instructions or in keeping patient records.

Private-duty nurses and visiting nurses need to be subjective to enjoy working with individual patients, while those who aim for supervisory positions should be objective. Among objective graduate nurses measured by the Laboratory are a head of a woman's hospital, a clinic manager, a superintendent of hospital wards, an executive secretary of a social welfare group, and a state director of nurses' training.

The human engineers believe that more girls who are thinking seriously of becoming nurses should instead consider becoming doctors, that girls too often think of themselves as assisting someone rather than doing the work themselves. They would like to see more women with high structural visualization and inductive reasoning enter medicine.

Dental hygiene is another profession that attracts women. The dental hygienist needs the same aptitudes as a dentist; that is, subjective personality, high structural visualization, tweezer dexterity and low ideaphoria. The same pattern in general applies to laboratory technicians. And it would seem that the various aides and para-professionals probably would need aptitudes similar to the professionals they assist.

There are numerous fields closely allied to medicine where those with a high medical vocabulary can be of important use. For example, a person with a sales aptitude pattern might work to promote public health and modern medical knowledge; the executive can perform many of the administrative and executive jobs in public health. Raising funds for research, managing hospitals and hospitalization plans are only a few of the places he can be of real use. Public health inspectors are becoming more important as people grow aware of health problems. Their primary aptitude is observation. And certainly pollution and its effect on physical and mental health is yet another challenge for the public health official.

In these fields so directly concerned with our physical and mental health, knowledge assumes great importance. All doctors need high vocabulary in addition to a vast and growing knowledge in their specializations. One unhappy doctor tested by the Laboratory had taken to drinking heavily. He proved to have a low vocabulary. The human engineers find that very often people who have the aptitudes for a job but don't know enough to do it well become heavy drinkers.

It is the high vocabulary doctor who can recognize the importance of psychology in the treatment of the ill. Certainly psychosomatic medicine confirms what a vital part the mind plays in many of our ailments. But beyond that, wide knowledge helps the doctor take a broad viewpoint on life which he needs for perspective about the individual tragedies in his work. The rapid advances in medical knowledge demand that the doctor keep abreast of the latest findings in his specialty or fall behind.

Probably few careers offer more personal satisfaction. But to gain this satisfaction, natural abilities coupled with hard work to acquire skill and knowledge is of utmost importance.

9

The Teacher

Most of us would agree that education is, or should be, a training for living, the foundation we need for the fullest self-development, and the means through which we can find our place in society. The more we learn, the better prepared we are to get along in life. The great educator Horace Mann said, "Education alone can conduct us to that enjoyment which is, at once, best in quality and infinite in quantity."

Much of our desire to learn is instilled in us by our teachers and their influence can be far-reaching. Henry Adams believed that "a teacher affects eternity; he can never tell where his influence stops." A good teacher helps us not only to learn but inspires us to want to learn more. A poor teacher may so discourage us that ambition, confidence and intellectual curiosity are thwarted rather than stimulated, and it may take years to undo the damage, with many never inspired to seek further learning.

There are a great many good teachers, devoted men and women who excel in their work. But there are others who, for their own sakes and for that of their students, do not belong in teaching at all. It takes more than a desire to teach and a degree in education to make a good teacher. The Laboratory has found that the most successful and effective teachers, and the ones who get the greatest satisfaction from teaching, have a definite aptitude pattern. The combination is high ideaphoria, inductive reasoning, abstract visualization and objective personality. Roughly, about one woman in twenty-eight and one man in forty-three have this combination of aptitudes. In Laboratory parlance, this is a "group-influencing" pattern that politicians, advertisers and promoters also have. Certainly teaching is a group-influencing job, for a teacher must have the ability to instill learning in the students and inspire interest and enthusiasm for it.

The top trait of a good teacher is ideaphoria. An old Greek proverb says, "A schoolmaster spends his life telling the same people the same things about the same things." A teacher needs an abundant flow of ideas, to formulate new projects and stimulating assignments to keep the students interested. The teacher who lacks the trait usually fails at teaching; too often he leads a dull and bored class. And unless he has the aptitude, he, too, can fall into a rut teaching the same things over and over in the same way. The satirist Juvenal put it this way: "It is repetition, like cabbage served at every meal, that wears out the schoolmaster's life."

But ideaphoria by itself is not enough. In any work, unless there is another strong aptitude to guide it, it can run wild. In teaching, particularly beyond kindergarten and the first or second grade, inductive reasoning is necessary as the controlling aptitude. While ideaphoria enables the teacher to think of a wide variety of lesson plans, inductive reasoning is necessary to analyze what the student already knows, and to discard those approaches not applicable to his present knowledge. Without inductive reasoning, the high-ideaphoria teacher too often gets impatient with those pupils slow to grasp what he is trying to teach, and fails to make certain a student understands the lesson before moving on to something new. A student stands still when instruction is above or below his knowledge level, and it takes high inductive reasoning by a teacher to grasp the student's level and teach or assign work accordingly. To thoroughly learn, a student must build knowledge systematically. A few teachers do not need inductive reasoning, such as primary school and music teachers, and those who instruct by demonstration.

In general teaching, however, inductive reasoning is essential, and the high-ideaphoria teacher who lacks the trait can do more harm than good to his students because of this inability to link the new with what the student knows. And the teacher himself is inclined to be abnormally restless, often shifting from one school to another and constantly nagged by a persistent desire for change.

One man, who has the high ideaphoria—low inductive problem, has been teaching in private schools for some years, moving from one school to another. As soon as he has settled in one place he wants to be somewhere else. Until recently, he had no trouble selling himself as a teacher, for he has looks, charm, a high vocabulary and an impressive educational background. He enjoys the quick, easy-to-teach students and writes off those who can't grasp what he is trying to teach as stupid and hopeless.

Now approaching middle-age and more restless than ever, he is finding school doors closed to him, partly because of his record of moving so much, but mainly because he lacks the reputation of a good teacher. He has perfect sales aptitudes, and the human engineers have tried to tell him he should sell in some high vocabulary field, possibly fine antiques because they are his hobby. But he refuses. He feels such work is beneath him and uses his high vocabulary to rationalize his behavior. He has become a rover, picking up odd jobs and rapidly going down hill.

Because teaching deals essentially with ideas and theories, high abstract visualization rather than structural ability characterizes the most successful teachers. The Laboratory has found that this appears to be true even among science teachers. If a teacher does possess structural visualization, he needs to score higher in ideaphoria and inductive reasoning to teach effectively. Perhaps Goethe had this in mind when he wrote, "A teacher who can arouse a feeling for one single action, for one single good poem, accomplishes more than he who fills our memory with rows and rows of natural objects, classified with name and form." But beyond this, the teacher with structural visualization as his strongest aptitude is not happy teaching, for he gets little opportunity to use it.

At the pre-college level, the best teachers are objective. For one thing, the objective person enjoys working with groups and the subjective does not. But perhaps the main drawback is the problem of discipline, and a subjective teacher in a classroom packed with assorted types of students too often can spell chaos. Because he is naturally sensitive, he takes things to heart, and so can be an open target for those students who inevitably try to get the upper hand. The objective person has fewer discipline problems, for he can ignore or slough off many matters that upset the subjective and he can also establish greater rapport with the students because of his outgoing nature.

Many subjectives are drawn into teaching because they like children and although this inclination is important, it can be misleading. Not long ago, a very attractive young fourth-grade teacher came to the Tulsa Laboratory to take the tests. She was nervous, upset and seemed on the verge of tears. When asked if something was wrong, she broke down and tearfully told her story.

After teaching for three years, she had just been dismissed from her job for incompetence. "I knew myself that I was not a good teacher," she said, "and I had come to hate it, but I didn't think it showed. I can't understand what happened to me. I had always dreamed of becoming a teacher. To me it seemed such a noble profession and one where I could do something for humanity. And Mom and Dad always said I must be a born teacher because I had such a way with children. People always wanted me to babysit because their kids were so crazy about me and I love children. We would make things together and have lots of fun. But then," she continued, "when I actually started teaching everything seemed to go wrong. I tried so hard but I couldn't get the little monsters to mind me and the discipline in my class was the worst in the whole school. But the worst was that I couldn't seem to get the kids to learn and I knew it in my heart, but it still was an awful blow to learn that the school authorities knew it, too. They told me when they fired me that many parents had complained that their kids weren't learning anything."

She proved to have aptitudes the exact opposite of a good teacher; extremely subjective, 100 per cent structural visualization, and no ideaphoria or inductive reasoning. When it was explained to her why she had failed as a teacher, and where her talents lay in technical or structural work, her relief was apparent. Since she had high observation— teachers score low in this—and both hand dexterities, work as a laboratory technician or possibly in engineering was suggested to her. She left the Laboratory in high spirits, determined to start using her real abilities and stop worrying about her teaching failure.

College teachers often are subjective and enjoy their work. But they are unlikely to have classroom discipline problems, and they have more opportunity to work with the individual student. Usually they teach a specialty, with time to pursue it on their own. Many teach while working for doctorates, planning to continue teaching their field of concentration. A danger is that their specialization may be too narrow to give breadth and perspective to their teaching, especially in some areas of science and the humanities. Some college officials recognize this, and some universities are enlarging the scope of doctoral work to include more emphasis on teaching skills.

The subjective teacher with high ideaphoria, inductive reasoning and abstract visualization has writer's aptitudes, and a college teaching career often is greatly enhanced by the publication of articles and books. He also can give effective lecture courses in his specialty, for ideaphoria, inductive reasoning, and perhaps analytical reasoning are needed to give sparkle, interest and well-arranged subject matter to his talks. Many of us can remember college instructors whose lectures were a dull stringing together of dry facts that made it hard to stay awake, and others who kept us so stimulated we hung on every word.

The best school administrators need to have the typical executive aptitude pattern of objectivity, low ideaphoria, usually low inductive reasoning and high abstract visualization. Yet, as mentioned before, too often the best teachers are the ones promoted to administrative jobs where they seldom are content, and neither are the teachers under their direction.

Some years ago, a delightful older man, dean of the Agricultural Department of a large western state university, took the Laboratory's tests shortly before he planned to retire. He proved to have the ideal executive aptitudes and a very high vocabulary. During his long teaching career, he had preferred his administrative work far more. He agreed with the human engineers about what constituted a teacher's aptitudes and recognized his own failings as a teacher and his success as an executive. He said that the university students rate the faculty on two things: knowledge of their subject and the ability to put it over. He said he always got "A" for knowledge, and "D" for communication.

He had sought help from the human engineers to find out what he should do after retirement. As he put it, he had no desire to "try to grow the biggest tomatoes in the county." He was urged not to retire completely but to continue to use his executive ability and wide agricultural knowledge. Several years later, he wrote to the Laboratory. He said he had retired from his old job, but that his so-called retirement now consisted of serving as vice-president of the university, and devoting much of his time to helping farmers in the state increase production of a particular farm product. The effectiveness of his work was revealed in a number of newspaper clippings enclosed in his letter. The stories gave high praise for his work, saying that he was largely responsible for bringing fame to the state for that product.

To a teacher in the lower grades, graphoria may not be essential since there are few papers to correct. But in the higher grades it makes the job of marking papers easier. The human engineers have found that high school teachers average above the median in the aptitude. And while this helps the teacher, too often it can prove detrimental to some students.

In almost any class there are some students who are low graphoria, but most teachers make assignments based on their own accounting aptitude. Because they can complete an assignment in a certain length of time, they reason the students can do likewise. What they fail to realize is that what they can do in an hour can take the low-graphoria student as much as five hours. Too frequently he gets discouraged with school, falls behind in his work, and loses self-confidence. Often he is scolded by both parents and teachers, accused of laziness, of not applying himself, when the truth is only that allowance must be made for the extra time it takes him to finish an assignment. This could well be one reason the high school dropout rate is so high. The low-graphoria student needs as much individual attention as he can get, but with big classes it is almost impossible for a teacher to do this. For this reason, the Laboratory recommends that whenever possible low-graphoria children should attend small schools, for their chances of receiving more individual attention are far greater.

Because education is so important, and because our teachers exert so much influence on our lives, they need not only to have the right aptitudes for teaching, but they need high vocabulary. The teacher who can inspire in his students the need for a wide knowledge of the world and its peoples performs a valuable service, for he helps to improve the quality of life. A high vocabulary enables him to take a broad view of life and sort out what is important to teach from masses of facts. The human engineers find that college teachers score higher in vocabulary than preparatory and high school teachers, while elementary ones are lower still.

But a startling and disturbing fact has come to light in a recent Laboratory study. Fifteen percent of high school students at ages fifteen and sixteen score higher in vocabulary than the average high school teacher. What inspiration can such students get? Is it any wonder so many become bored and restless, even rebellious, or lack respect for their teachers? College teachers are also often low in vocabulary in comparison with many of their students. The result is a lack of communication, boredom on the part of high-vocabulary students, and a dissatisfaction that can take many forms including dropping out of college, a loss of respect for teachers and authority, and possibly the widespread campus unrest.

We are fortunate to have many high-vocabulary, dedicated teachers. But the human engineers are finding that more and more of them, particularly in the high schools, are leaving the profession for other work. They may have ideal aptitudes for teaching and enjoy it above all else, but they have a number of reasons for leaving. One commonly given is the difficulty of working under their supervisors. But the most frequent reason is not the students but the other teachers with whom they are associated. Because of vocabulary difference, they don't speak the same language and can find little in common. To find our friends we gravitate towards those with vocabulary levels similar to our own.

Another reason high-vocabulary teachers leave teaching —and this may surprise you—is school architecture. Too many schools are monotonous and dreary with long corridors that lead to equally uninspiring classrooms which are not only inconvenient and impractical, but offer little esthetic pleasure. A third, but less frequent reason for leaving teaching is the desire to earn more money. And undoubtedly higher salaries would draw more high-vocabulary teachers into the profession.

Because today's frontier is knowledge, education has vast importance. It is through education that we can raise the quality of life and abolish the ignorance that constitutes a major human problem.

10

The Researcher

Since earliest times, intellectual curiosity has spurred man on to an unrelenting search for truth, for a greater knowledge of the universe and its phenomena. Research projects start with the exhilarating ambition of solving world problems, of lessening man's miseries, and gradually give mankind more understanding of itself and the world about.

Although there are many types of research, that of science has had an enormous impact on our lives. Names of great men of science stand out throughout history. Yet it wasn't until Francis Bacon influenced thinking from medieval theorizing to observation, experimentation, and measurement that foundations were laid for applying scientific research to material advantage. From research have come the great discoveries that underlie the standard of living we now take for granted.

Research is cumulative—a step-by-step process that can bring about dramatic changes. For example, think of the research involved in enabling a man to walk on the moon; of how research into molecules and atoms has brought us plastics and other synthetics; of the recent isolation of a gene and what it can mean to future genetic research and man's understanding of his makeup. We have only to look around us to realize the vast impact of research on our lives.

The growth of almost any enterprise springs from research, creating whole new industries and occupations. And while it is basic research that produces the great discoveries, it is industrial research that finds social and economic applications.

Today there is a special opportunity for scientific researchers to undertake almost any kind of research and thereby earn a living—a far cry from the days when a person experimenting in a rough, home-made laboratory was often looked upon as eccentric. Universities, the great foundations, government and industrial laboratories, and institutions of many kinds have given the dedicated research worker opportunities to pursue his work to an extent unheard of only a few decades ago. Vast sums of money are allocated to research and development, and the true researcher at long last has come into his own.

The world today admires the researcher. Interesting evidence of this has come to light through one of the Laboratory's vocabulary tests. In the test, the word *luminary* is included, meaning any person who enlightens mankind, a dignitary, a celebrity, a star. The five choices of words from which to choose the one that comes closest in meaning include *researcher* and *celebrity,* the latter used here as the correct answer. Yet more people pick *researcher* as a luminary than a celebrity. It is true that a researcher, if successful, may enlighten the world, but many hard workers spend a lifetime searching only to find little or nothing. Yet because the true meaning of luminary is one who lights the way for humanity, it is significant that people associate it with research.

The key aptitude for scientific research is structural visualization coupled with subjective personality. It is this three-dimensional thinking, problem-solving aptitude that enables the physical chemist to synthesize complicated crystals from organic molecules and unseen atoms, that enables the geologist to establish mountain slopes from contour lines on a two-dimensional map. Subjectivity is essential because of the often isolated nature of the work, and the ability of the subjective person to pursue his work with a singleness of aim and purpose.

Almost any scientist must have inductive reasoning. He must be able to put isolated observations together and formulate a new generalization. Some, such as medical researchers, need also to have analytical reasoning to resolve an idea into its component parts. If the work involves using a microscope or other activities that require an ability to notice changes immediately, the observation aptitude is important. If the work includes picking up objects with the fingers or handling small tools, finger and/or tweezer dexterity is necessary.

As a rule, research scientists should lack ideaphoria to be able to stick to one thing and not go off on tangents. For some reason, the human engineers are finding that the music aptitude, pitch discrimination, is almost as important to the scientist as structural visualization. It may be that the aptitude enables him to be more perceptive. Language learning, as measured by the Laboratory's silograms test, seems to be a top trait of chemists, and certainly they must remember a great many unfamiliar words. The researcher needs to have foresight to be able to keep a distant goal in mind and not give up in discouraging moments. And it goes without saying that they need high vocabulary, both general and in their specialized fields.

Structural visualization is, of course, the all-important aptitude for scientific research. Men inherit the ability from their mothers; women from either parent. It is believed to be an inherited, sex-linked recessive trait. There is strong evidence that all natural mental traits come in pairs, somewhat of the nature of equivalent (allelomorphic) pairs in genetics. For example, color blindness is inherited and sex-linked. The Laboratory cannot measure color blindness but it can measure color perception, and a low score indicates color blindness. In the case of structural visualization, a low test score points to superior ability to think in tangible terms, which the human engineers call abstract visualization. Men surpass women in structural visualization, but women outdo men in abstract thinking.

Perhaps the fact that a son never inherits structural visualization from his father is the reason why we hear of no great scientific dynasties such as we find in business, politics, diplomacy and the like, where family career tradition continues through generations. And who knows how much heartache and mental suffering have been caused by sons being forced to follow in traditional family footsteps?

Some years ago, the son of a business-minded family was tested. The parents, who led a very active social life, said they could not understand him. He was unsocial, always had his nose in a book, and couldn't care less about the family business, an old established multi-million dollar corporation in which they took great pride. They were certain something must be wrong with him and thought perhaps the tests might offer some clue as to his behavior and help him change his ways.

The son tested extremely subjective with very high structural visualization and the other aptitudes ideal for scientific research. But the father, a forceful and domineering type, scoffed at the whole idea. In the first place, he was positive his son was not subjective, but only shy, and he certainly couldn't see his son becoming a scientist. It was the tradition in the family, he said, for the sons to continue the business, and that tradition was not about to change because of any tests.

The son did go into the family business, rose to become a vice-president after six years, and then quit. For awhile he worked in a large bank, which also was work the exact opposite of his aptitudes. He now lives in a home for mental cases. His story, with varying alterations, including suicides, could be repeated many times in the Laboratory's records. To be ourselves we must be true to our born personality, not always easy in a world where objectivity and good fellowship is the accepted pattern.

Maladjustment can start early in childhood. If both parents are subjective, the subjective youngster grows up in an environment where individualism is encouraged and he rarely has problems later. But the lone subjective child in an objective family can be another story unless the parents understand his nature. With all good intentions, many parents who are out-going themselves, try to bring out their own qualities in their retiring, self-absorbed youngster. They may scold and criticize him for unsocial behavior, and too often push him into objective activities that can bring him to the threshold of a nervous breakdown, or an assortment of emotional problems. Other than learning good manners and certain social graces, this child should be allowed to be his subjective self and encouraged to make his own unique contribution.

One such boy, a budding young scientist, was tested recently. His story is unusual and, in a sense, amusing, but it points up sharply the difference between objective and subjective behavior. His family had decided to combine taking the Laboratory's tests and sightseeing in New York at the same time. The trip involved a four-hour train ride, and the family arrived at the station early, allowing plenty of time for all the last-minute details involved in taking three children on a trip. They were in an excited holiday mood, laughing and talking so much that it wasn't until they were boarding the train that they were aware that their quiet twelve-year-old boy was not with them.

At first they were not too concerned. They knew he was a resourceful loner who often wandered off by himself or shut himself up in his room, absorbed in his science books and messy flora and fauna. They thought he had managed to board the train ahead of them and would appear at any moment. But as they neared New York and there was no sign of him, the father finally discovered that he was not on the train at all. The family arrived at the New York Laboratory in great alarm, anxious to call home to see if he had returned there. But the boy himself greeted them. He had slipped off while they were talking and had taken an earlier train. The worksamples showed him to be extremely subjective with brilliant science research aptitudes; the others in the family all tested extremely objective. He confided in the test administrator about taking a different train. "I just couldn't bear," he said, "the thought of being cooped up for four hours with that noisy bunch of yakkers."

Because of their subjectivity, most research scientists work quietly behind the scenes. They are the "back room" men and women, who generally remain anonymous except when some major discovery is announced or an award such as the Nobel Prize is given. As a rule, they shun publicity and are cautious in disclosing findings. The subjective person often lacks faith in himself and needs bolstering up and encouragement.

Many of the projects worked on by research scientists can seem preposterous or unsound to others. The "mad scientist" of fiction with his fantastic creations is, of course, a wild exaggeration, but may in a sense be indicative of public opinion. Because he is alone in the world with his special problem which may take years to be solved, he may have to confront a world that doesn't understand him. He needs wide knowledge to enhance self-confidence and make his work effective, knowledge not only in his particular field, but of the world in general.

Even though subjectives are a minority, subjective men with strong structural visualization have few problems if they select a structural profession. But the subjective woman equally gifted, and even more of a minority, too often expects to fail and rarely goes into scientific research as a career. There are, of course, exceptions, and there are women who have made and are making outstanding contributions. But too often the scientifically-gifted girl avoids science courses. One woman, now in her forties and deeply involved in a national research project, says she deliberately avoided science in high school, mainly because she was afraid her school friends would think she was odd. Now she says she would give anything to have acquired a background in the exact sciences at a time when this might have been gained so easily.

The human engineers maintain that if we are subjective and have strong structural visualization, we need to build a solid background in physics, chemistry and mathematics if our interests are in the sciences.

The importance of finger or tweezer dexterity in certain kinds of scientific research should not be underestimated. The need for such a skill may seem trivial, but it can prove to be a serious stumbling block. One well-known chemist now doing significant work, almost abandoned chemistry because of the lack of this very trait. He had become excessively nervous and felt he was on the verge of a breakdown, yet his doctors could find nothing to explain his condition. Although he preferred chemistry to any other work, he had decided it must in some way be causing his problem, and he wanted help from the Laboratory to decide what else he could do.

He proved to have ideal aptitudes for his work, but he scored as low as one can in tweezer dexterity. He saw his problem immediately and said he never had been so relieved in his life. He explained then that much of his work over the years had involved picking up minute particles with a small instrument and shifting their positions, which would, of course, demand strong tweezer dexterity. With this self-knowledge, he decreased his laboratory work, but when this type of work is necessary he has an assistant to handle equipment. This one small adjustment has made a world of difference to him.

Sometimes an objective person has a strong desire to do research, and wants to be connected with an important project. Such persons can serve as mediators between a research laboratory and the outside world. For instance, they can publicize, raise funds, administrate, and do many things that only annoy the research worker.

And what about the objective person with both a strong interest and a solid background in science who wants both research and administrative work? An interesting case came to light recently when a man brought his three sons to one of the Laboratories to take the tests. He himself had been tested in the Thirties and brought his scores with him. His aptitudes were objectivity, high structural visualization, inductive reasoning, ideaphoria, observation, graphoria, finger and tweezer dexterity and high vocabulary.

He said he had taken his master's degree in chemistry, extra work in physics, and began his career in purely subjective research. During the war he did chemical research for the Army. His present job, which he says gives him more satisfaction than ever before, combines research with administrative work. He heads an important project significant to the space program. He has twelve patents to his credit—inventors have high structural visualization and ideaphoria. The interesting part is that he not only is the man in charge, but also has the opportunity to use his structural visualization.

In testing many young persons today, the human engineers are encountering a serious problem with those who have the ideal traits for scientific research. Many refuse even to consider it as a career because they are convinced any discovery they would make would be used for military purposes, and they want no part of it. A Harvard student recently tested has everything he would need for scientific research, including a very high vocabulary, but will not enter a research profession for this reason. No one can deny that many research discoveries have been and are being used for war purposes, but there are a great many that are not which are of enormous benefit to mankind. Halting research will not stop wars; only people can do that.

Of course not all research is scientific. For the subjective, research-oriented persons with abstract visualization there are many possibilities. There is no field where discoveries are not possible. The subjective personality with almost any aptitude pattern can fit into research. Statistical research, for example, is based almost entirely on graphoria; historical research leans heavily on inductive reasoning and, if creative writing is involved, ideaphoria. One type of work often classified as research that requires an objective personality is mass interviewing, where information is acquired by talking to people. But in general, the objective person does not fit happily into research work which in reality is the realm of the subjectives.

This is not meant to imply that all extremely subjective persons should be researchers, for there are many other careers from which to choose. It is only that any subjective person is happiest doing individual, specialized work that he can do in his own way. And often at heart the crusader, the missionary, the explorer or leader, the deeply subjective person wants to make a unique contribution to mankind.

11

The Office Worker

Most organizations lean heavily on a competent office staff. While it is true that machines may perform much of the clerical drudgery, the human being remains an integral part of any office. No computer can as yet feed itself; the "speedy idiot" can do only what it is told to do. But when programmed properly, it is a miraculous time and labor saver, coping with clerical tasks that otherwise would be overwhelming or even impossible. The machines' elimination of many clerical jobs may well be a good thing. Why devote a life to a tedious menial job that a machine can do better and faster?

In office jobs, the key aptitude is graphoria, or accounting ability. It is essential to secretaries, stenographers, typists, key punch operators, clerks, data processors, bookkeepers, office managers, accountants, statisticians, programmers and the like for accuracy, speed and enjoyment of work. Those low in the aptitude make mistakes, and are inclined to be slow and fall behind in their work. Above all, they are not happy doing the work because it is not natural to them. More women than men have the aptitude—75 per cent of women score as high as 50 per cent of men. This may be one reason we find more women than men in office jobs. But very few persons score at the very top in the aptitude.

In a group of 500 employees, there might be five who score 100 per cent in it.

The type of personality needed for office work depends on the particular job. For most routine jobs, subjectivity may be the most desirable. To spend hours typing, running machines, or poring over accounts and doing other solitary work, we must enjoy working alone. The objective person gets restless and craves companionship; he or she wants to visit and may waste too much time talking to co-workers or telephoning friends so that the work doesn't get done promptly.

On the other hand, office managers and supervisors, secretaries and receptionists are objective, for their work involves working and dealing with others. Programmers may have either personality; when their work interrelates with that of others, they may need objectivity.

The only other aptitude besides graphoria really needed for most office jobs is finger dexterity, for clumsy fingers can be a great deterrent. Actually, to be content in their jobs, most office workers are happiest with only these aptitudes. Other unused aptitudes only increase boredom and restlessness.

An exception is the private secretary, who also needs to have high inductive reasoning. Her job is a responsible one, for often she must carry on alone while the boss is away. In one day, she may be called upon to make numerous small decisions whose content she has never encountered before, and for decision-making she needs inductive reasoning.

The file clerk may need number memory. You will recall that this aptitude means not only ease in remembering numbers, but an ability to keep many things in one's mind. Although this ability helps the file clerk find a particular item more readily, it also can have its drawbacks. Because she herself knows where she puts things, the file clerk may have a classification system which is a mystery to anyone else. Who hasn't had this experience? The author was once madly searching through a huge picture morgue for a photo of a cow. The secretary in charge was busy but finally after a long and futile search under every possible heading, she was asked where cows would be. "Oh," she replied, "that would be under 'Female.'"

In addition to graphoria, programmers need inductive and analytical reasoning, number memory, and perhaps structural visualization. The latter is useful in structuring situations to make a flow chart. But most office workers need abstract visualization rather than structural ability. In banking, where graphoria is the primary trait, the human engineers have found structural visualization is a handicap and abstract visualization essential. In fact, some banks who use the Laboratory's services generally find new structural jobs with various depositers for employees who test high in structural visualization.

As mentioned earlier, for any office job graphoria is the aptitude most needed. Its lack, you may recall, underlies many school problems. Paradoxically, many girls who, because they lack graphoria, may have had discouraging school experiences, or even flunked out of college, turn to office job training to be on their own. But whether they are good in their work, and enjoy it, is another story. The Laboratory tests many such girls who, after the enthusiasm for a first job has worn off, are disheartened. Invariably they test with low graphoria but with other strong aptitudes they should be developing and using.

Failure in a first job too often leaves an otherwise brilliantly gifted girl with strong feelings of inferiority that may kill incentive to set sights higher, and aim for work more in keeping with her true aptitudes and interests. It takes courage and hard work to rise above the humiliation of an unsatisfactory work performance in a first job. And it is so easy to label a person carelessly as impossible because he lacks competence in his job. Many of us grew up believing that we should be able to do almost anything if we put our backs into it and tried hard enough. This is not so; we are limited by our inborn aptitudes. We may acquire a certain skill in something unnatural to us, but we never feel right within, nor can we really compete with those who have better aptitudes. In times of stress or pressure, our acquired skills often desert us, and we panic.

Several years ago, an extremely attractive girl came to the Los Angeles Laboratory to take the worksamples. She had just resigned as secretary in a large company, saying to the test administrator that she just couldn't stand it another day. It was dull; she was criticized constantly for making mistakes; and although she had tried hard to be friendly with her co-workers, she felt that they did not really accept her and she was uncomfortable with them. She was beginning to think it was hopeless, and that something must be wrong with her.

She was a college graduate who had majored in music, specializing in piano, but felt she was not good enough to perform professionally. Because she didn't want to teach music and didn't know what else to do, she had taken secretarial training. She proved to be objective with low graphoria, high ideaphoria, high in the art and music aptitudes, and had a vocabulary on a level with top executives. With this self-knowledge the source of many of her problems became clear. She lacked the graphoria needed for both secretarial work and for playing the piano—this aptitude is needed for rapid reading of music written in two clefs. To be a performer, she would need to be subjective. Her high ideaphoria would make her rebel at routine work and all these traits, coupled with a vocabulary far above her work associates, made it obvious why she felt as she did.

When the test administrator pointed out that her combination of aptitudes indicated executive work in music, possibly theater management, she became enthusiastic and excited. But where to begin? The whole idea seemed so impossible. Yet further discussion revealed that most of her close friends were involved in the theater, and she had taken an active part in college theatricals. She had loved this work and still kept in touch with the people involved. She decided to find a small college which might let her start a little theater. It was a bold, difficult venture, but she is now well on her way.

Many girls take secretarial jobs in the hope that they will lead to bigger and better jobs. For some this may be true but it is rarely the case. For one thing, if you are a good secretary, you become so indispensable few officials would be willing to let you go. And too often the title of secretary sticks with you. The Laboratory believes that women who aspire to more professional careers do best to start directly with the kind of work they ultimately want, even if it means beginning with the lowliest kind of a job. When the Laboratory tested one hundred women with distinguished careers, only three knew stenography and typing, and only one had started out via the typewriter.

As anyone who works knows, few offices are free of complaints, petty jealousies, and gossiping. Some of this is just human nature, but much is caused by the pressure of unused aptitudes. A person busy and interested in his own work doesn't have time to be bothered with such nonsense. Much of the problem lies with boredom, for most office jobs, especially in large organizations, do not offer enough variety, and a girl may be hired to perform a single routine job.

Some office managers have found partial solutions to the problem. The supervisor of a secretarial pool in a large chemical company wrote to me after reading one of my books on the Laboratory's work: "I did a multitude of experiments trying to solve the problem of boredom. The girls were all college graduates or from secretarial schools with college credits. From this group were selected candidates for the private secretarial positions throughout the company. We started a circulating library, we had horseback rides, played golf, badminton, and even a group for sketching and painting. The girls took turns managing the office with full responsibility for a week. One of the most amazing results was that girls often turned down promotions to private offices and sometimes asked to be transferred back because they were so lonesome in a private office." Obviously, these girls were objective and their technical bosses undoubtedly subjective.

Most secretaries need to be objective, for their work usually involves maintaining good public relations. But in an effort to conform to the typical secretary image, some subjective secretaries try to behave objectively and the inner conflict can be disastrous. One woman who had been the private secretary to a prominent business executive wrote me how relieved she had been to learn from the tests that she was extremely subjective. Her letter says in part, "Previously I had supposed that the objective personality was the normal one, and had expended constant effort and grazed the edges of two nervous breakdowns in fruitless effort to change my extremely subjective nature, the constant resurgence of which I feared was an early sign of insanity. To find that such a temperament is perfectly normal is like having my life given me to live over again."

While for most office jobs, from clerk to accountant, the ideal aptitude pattern is graphoria, subjectivity, finger dexterity and little else, other strong aptitudes are almost certain to be present in most people. But even if graphoria is the only strong trait, it can be used to build an interesting career, the choice influenced by the type of personality. If objective and with wide knowledge, one could find executive work the answer; if subjective, one could go far in accounting or in statistical research. But if we have other strong aptitudes, and most of us do, we belong in a corresponding field, for the chances are far greater for opportunity to develop it. Also, in doing office work in a congenial atmosphere, we not only learn, but feel more at home in it, for we find more fellow workers who share our interests and tastes.

If you have low graphoria there is nothing you can do to change it. It seems to be inborn, fixed by inheritance and unchanged by experience. A saving grace for many who lack this accounting aptitude is that today machines, even in banks, do much of the routine clerical work. To those low in the ability, but who must have office jobs or who really enjoy office atmospheres, the Laboratory suggests: If you have low accounting aptitude, push yourself, for speed and accuracy go together. The slow-but-sure plodder does not exist. You will still make mistakes but fewer than if you go slowly. Do the job from beginning to end. Do not stop in the middle to check. You probably have made no mistakes, but may make one when you start again. After you finish the entire assignment, but not before, check back for errors.

This technique is, of course, a compensatory one, but it

is highly useful to any low-graphoria person tackling paper-work of any kind. But for those who plan an office work career that hinges on accounting aptitude, graphoria is imperative for lasting satisfaction. Without it, the objective person can become an executive if he builds vocabulary, but the subjective cannot advance and needs to develop another specialty based on his strong aptitudes.

12

The Factory Worker

Probably most of us have days when "the world is too much with us," when we deplore industrialization and urbanization and daydream wistfully of the simple life. You might say the Thoreau in us comes out and we yearn for a Walden. But when it comes to everyday living, few of us would want to forego our material comforts and we're grateful for mass production and for the multitude of factory workers who make our standard of living possible.

So far as working conditions, benefits and wages are concerned, factory workers in general are better off than ever before. Also, modern equipment and automation have released many workers from back-breaking labor and from many tedious jobs along the production line. Yet strikes, work slow-downs, and general labor unrest indicate that something is wrong in our industrial life. Many strikes, of course, are justified and certainly money and better working conditions are important. But when these are achieved and dissatisfaction remains, the sources of discontent must lie deeper. The human engineers believe that unused aptitudes are in large part responsible, for most factory jobs by their very nature use only one or two aptitudes. Those workers more gifted, or those in work for which they lack the aptitude, are certain to be restless and unhappy.

From its findings over the years, the Laboratory is convinced that each person must exercise every aptitude he possesses, and that failure in life checks not so much with a lack of endowments as with too many. The industrial restlessness derived from the frustration of unused aptitudes breaks out in strikes and protests about working conditions, management decisions and wages. And money appears to be the least important grievance, for vice-presidents and others at high salary levels have appeared for the Laboratory's tests with almost exactly the same complaints and criticisms. Strikes are not only expensive and wasteful but so detrimental to good labor relations that everything possible should be done to reduce their occurrence.

Years ago a factory worker could expect to be out of a job every twenty years as his type of work became obsolescent. Today, this happens in ten or twelve years as new skills are needed and machines take over many jobs. But machines replace only the low-vocabulary, unskilled jobs; as yet no machine can replace a high-vocabulary one. Even if one is only at the 17th percentile in vocabulary, no machine can take over his job. Many factory jobs require the same aptitudes; the difference in the individual's progress rests with vocabulary. For example, machinists score higher in vocabulary than mechanics. Thus, to step up to a machinists job a mechanic's vocabulary needs to be improved to that level. Factory workers must increase their vocabulary if they expect promotion. Unions and management can do much to help workers be ready to move up.

A large factory can use almost any combination of aptitudes. For assembly workers, the trait most needed is finger dexterity. The test for finger dexterity, one of the first worksamples developed by the HEL, consists of a wooden board punched with one hundred holes, ten rows with ten holes to a row. At one end is a slight depression filled with more than three hundred steel pins. You are asked to put three pins in each hole, filling as many as you can within six minutes. Rarely does a person fill all the holes, but if he does, pins in the top rows are quickly removed so one can continue until the time is up. In testing employees of an electronics company that manufactures digital voltmeters, twenty-three out of one hundred and seventy persons filled one hundred or more holes. The top score of one hundred and twenty-two holes, which occurs about once every ten years in Laboratory testing, was made by a product designer.

Any work that requires skill in handling small tools needs tweezer dexterity, which is entirely different from finger dexterity. You can be adept at working with small tools but be all thumbs when it comes to working with your fingers. Tweezer dexterity is essential to the toolmaker, die-maker, airplane mechanic, those doing miniature instrument repair, and the like.

When the Laboratory first started, it was thought that for all manual jobs, including miniature instrument work, it was enough to have nimble fingers because we use the same fingers to handle an object as we do in using a tool. For quite some time those employees who made high scores in finger dexterity were placed in manual jobs, including miniature assembly. But something seemed wrong, and it took a clever forewoman in charge of training girls to challenge the theory and prove she was right.

She maintained that some persons naturally work better with small tools than do others. To prove her point, she placed a mass of tiny springs on a table, along with a tweezer, and then asked for the employment office to send in a girl applying for a job. When the girl was asked to untangle the mass, she tackled the snarled springs with her fingers. Two more girls were called in and did the same. But the fourth girl picked up the tweezers and went to work. This was the start of the tweezer dexterity worksample. It is similar to the finger dexterity one, except tweezers are used to pick up one hundred pins and place them in the holes. In general, women score higher than men in finger dexterity, but more men have tweezer dexterity.

Structural visualization is necessary to the mechanic, repairman, machinist and any worker whose job involves mechanical or structural work. Most factory workers are subjective, each intent on doing his own particular job. The objective person in such work may get lonesome and want to

ing to methods and procedures he knew from his experience in other printing plants were effective. But almost from the first day the plant manager had begun to interfere with his plans. He was inconsistent in his behavior and kept stirring up resentment among the shop men. One minute he would arouse anger in a worker by criticizing his work, and a few minutes later would slap him on the back and ask him how he was doing. The young foreman was driven to distraction. The plant manager would promise not to interfere, but no sooner were such promises made than the same meddling would begin. The foreman could take it no longer and resigned. It was then that he came to the Laboratory to take the worksamples. He had decided to become a specialist and wanted to know what line to follow.

He tested extremely objective with high memory for design, tweezer dexterity and average inductive reasoning —a pattern well suited for leading a group of skilled workers. To be a specialist he would need to be subjective. He decided to continue being a foreman but hopefully under a more objective, higher vocabulary plant manager.

For the worker who aspires to rise in factory work, there are many possibilities for advancement. An inspector, for example, needs the observation aptitude most of all. If what he inspects is mechanical, such as airplanes, automobiles or household appliances, he needs structural visualization. How many of us have had experience with "lemons" that never should have passed inspection! In recent years, the great number of automobiles recalled, often for re-inspection, is both costly to the company and devastating to the buyer, and could be lessened by starting with keener inspection.

Number memory enters into many factory jobs. In general, those in production control need objectivity with strong number memory. The chaser or expediter needs these traits as well as inductive reasoning and ideaphoria. And his job should not be underestimated, for the work of thousands can depend on him. He sees to it that materials arrive on schedule. One large plant, with an apparently poor expediter, had to lay off several thousand workers for ten weeks until an order for machine parts was delivered.

A production clerk sees that goods are delivered when promised. He needs number memory more than any other aptitude. Because he must keep involved accounts, it would seem that graphoria should be his strongest trait, but actually he always is ahead of written accounts and must keep many figures in his head.

A production planner needs number memory and executive aptitudes. When orders come in, his job is to forecast delivery dates. In an efficient plant, machines are scheduled far ahead and a competent production planner can predict almost exactly when an order can be delivered.

Much talent is going to waste in our factories. Many factory workers are held back by lack of education, urgent financial need, fear of taking risks that might jeopardize what job security they have, and by lack of faith in themselves and their abilities. A great many are held back by low vocabulary. Most but not all factory workers average low in vocabulary.

Several years ago, the Laboratory tested a worker who scored at the 95th percentile. He had started college but had to leave in his first year to help support the family. After holding a minor assembling and repairing job in a large automobile factory for seven years, he came for testing. Along with his unusually high vocabulary, he had a brilliant array of aptitudes—high structural visualization, ideaphoria, inductive reasoning, foresight, music aptitudes, low graphoria and extreme subjectivity. He had read my books on the Laboratory's work and wrote to me after he had been tested to tell me his story.

"My job was depressing and monotonous," he wrote, "and I felt myself capable of better things. I seemed out of step with my friends and coworkers although I have had more trouble repulsing companions than attracting them. I always have been an omnivorous reader and I had an unexplainable, to my friends, love for good music and serious books. I felt like a man who was shoulder deep in quicksand and had given up struggling."

The tests were a revelation to him. "I know now why I dislike figures, why I love symphonies, why I am good at solving problems in structure and how my high ideaphoria and vocabulary make me restless and wretched in the job I now hold."

The Laboratory had pointed out to him that his aptitudes and vocabulary indicated scientific research and writing, and suggested that he contact the head of a large research laboratory who knows the Laboratory's work well. He did this and was offered a research position and the opportunity to go back to college part-time. With new hope and faith in himself he is determined to succeed.

For the person with little education vocabulary building may seem a hopeless task. All too often he has too little knowledge to realize its importance, or even his own limitations in this respect.

A heartening story is that of a young man who, when tested at the age of twenty-two, was a ditch-digger. He scored at the 10th percentile in vocabulary and with executive and music aptitudes. He decided to really go to work on vocabulary, and when he came back to the Laboratory two years later to check his vocabulary, he did score somewhat higher. He had left ditch-digging and was now working in a factory as a lathe operator.

The next year his vocabulary had more than doubled and in two more years he had gone above the 50th percentile and was still studying. It is interesting to see how vocabulary growth was helping him raise his sights in life. After completing two years of high school, he is now in college, all of this schooling done after working hours. His ambition is to be an executive in radio or television. He says he is happier than ever before. Yet if he had not learned of his ability or had lacked the courage and willingness to build vocabulary, he probably would have continued either as ditch-digger or as a poor and dissatisfied lathe operator.

There is dignity in any job well done. There are many factory workers who truly like their work and have no desire for anything else. Certainly they have the satisfaction of knowing that their work is valuable. But for those who are restless and dissatisfied, raising vocabulary to take advantage of a chance to move up and a chance to use more of their true abilities could make a world of difference.

13

The Salesman

A common belief is that almost anyone can sell if he tries hard enough and learns the magic of turning on the charm. Dreams of high commissions, a chance to travel on an expense account, and a freedom from routine office work draw many into the selling field. This is especially true among those who have no special training and go into selling because they don't know what else to do. For some their careers work out very well and they are happy and successful. But too many find out as time goes on that selling is not for them. In a first spurt of enthusiasm and confidence, they may do well but then experience a gradual decline and feel inferior and dissatisfied as coworkers make more and better sales. Some develop nervous problems; others drink too much to bolster confidence; others quit to try something else. Some are such poor salesmen they are let go, left with feelings of failure often difficult to overcome, or, fortunately, are pushed into more suitable work. But the most unfortunate are those not poor enough to lose their jobs but who never get very far and hang on as dissatisfied, mediocre salesmen.

Those who make selling a lifetime career, who really enjoy it and are successful in it, fall into a definite aptitude pattern, a pattern that occurs only once in fifty-four persons.

This combination is objective personality, high ideaphoria, high abstract visualization, low inductive reasoning, low foresight and low vocabulary. Confirmation of this comes from a follow-up study of salesmen tested by the human engineers twenty or thirty years ago who have this pattern. All are high earners who thoroughly enjoy their work, and many so successful that they fly their own planes when they service far-off areas. As a result of this study, the human engineers have been able to establish an average score indicating satisfaction in sales. The HEL states that this coefficient of satisfaction is so unbelievably trustworthy that it should be followed almost categorically and that it predicts lasting and enjoyable achievement in selling with wholly unexpected precision. Actually, the coefficient is more important in eliminating areas for which we are not fitted than in selecting work.

Of all the aptitudes necessary for producing results, a salesman most needs ideaphoria for a rapid flow of ideas in his sales approaches. To get true satisfaction out of selling, the Laboratory says we should rarely attempt selling unless we have the aptitude in the highest degree. With less there is an abrupt decline in competence. Sales executives also have high ideaphoria but not so much as the direct salesman.

From the standpoint of the salesman himself, an objective personality is essential for lasting enjoyment in work that necessarily involves an almost constant dealing with people. The Laboratory once believed that the extremely objective person surpassed the lesser objective in selling, but the follow-up study shows this is not true. Either seems to do as well.

Because selling involves people and abstract ideas, the salesman needs high abstract visualization, even though the product sold may be based on structural concepts. An exception might be some types of sales engineering where solving structural problems is part of the job. But in most selling there is no opportunity to use structural visualization and unused high structure is a torment to its possessor.

The most effective salesmen lack inductive reasoning. It may be that the lack of this aptitude enables the salesman to be more persistent. He can keep his mind on one thing and not get sidetracked when a customer brings forth a new idea, for it takes him longer to grasp it than it does the person with high inductive reasoning. Also, high-inductive persons often love to argue and this, in turn, often can kill a sale. On the other hand, heads of merchandising, marketing and sales planning organizations score at the top in inductive reasoning. With few exceptions, they and sales managers have a high vocabulary, but the average salesman does not.

In fact, direct selling seems to be one place where we can have a low vocabulary and still make money. But this does not mean that all salesmen are deficient in vocabulary. Some are very high, but unless they are selling in a high vocabulary field, they rarely stay with it.

Career salesmen are not high in the foresight aptitude. Apparently they are more interested in the immediate sale than in the long-term goal. One man whose tests with perfect sales aptitudes refused a presidency, saying that he preferred the freedom and independence of selling to the heavy and endless responsibilities of the top man. The Laboratory believes that salesmen who do have strong foresight should establish their own business, or possibly become a manufacturer's representative.

It may be desirable for a salesman to have graphoria, for it is helpful in keeping records and accounts, but the Laboratory does not think it vital to success in sales and it is not included in the coefficient of satisfaction. After all, a successful salesman always can have someone else to do the paperwork for him.

Of all people, the subjective person does not belong in selling. The work can make him miserable and he seldom stays with it. Yet the paradoxical thing is when he does try selling, at first he can outsell the objective personalities. The reason may be that he is inclined to be more conscientious. The Laboratory finds that for a year or more the subjective salesman prospers surprisingly before deteriorating irretrievably, and then finds it too disrupting to readjust to the lower financial level needed to try again on a truly subjective course. After months of continuous unnatural pretense to an objective good fellowship, he ends too often with a serious nervous breakdown. Should subjective persons, the Laboratory believes, never sell even for a few months' experience, the number of emotional problems crowding our mental hospitals would drop perceptibly.

One man, tested in Fort Worth, sold advertising for a large public relations firm. At the time he was tested, he was excessively nervous, overweight, and a compulsive eater. Although only thirty-eight, he said for fifteen years he had consulted a doctor who could find no pathological cause for his nervousness. He scored 100 per cent subjective with high ideaphoria, high inductive reasoning, high abstract visualization and very high vocabulary. Despite making a great deal of money, he was most unhappy in his job and felt he was on the verge of a complete breakdown. When it was pointed out that his extreme subjective personality undoubtedly was the main cause of his problem and that he had been trying to be the opposite of his real self for years, he grasped the analysis immediately. His aptitudes were ideal for creative writing. He has moved from sales to the writing aspects of his business and is also writing on his own.

To be ourselves, we must be true to our individual personality. Scott's "Oh what a tangled web we weave, when first we practise to deceive!" is as true when we deceive ourselves as when we deceive others. And it was Montaigne who cautioned: "Follow the order of nature, for God's sake! Follow it! It will lead who follows and those who will not, it will drag along anyway, and their tempers and medicines with them."

We can't always tell by looks and actions if a person is objective or subjective, particularly if he has a high vocabulary. One man tested in Philadelphia appeared to be so much the sales type that the test administrator was positive he was extremely objective. But he proved to be 100 per cent subjective with low ideaphoria, high inductive reasoning, high abstract visualization, high foresight and high vocabulary. He had an impressive background in sales and management, and for ten years held a top position in a large corporation where his work included selling television programs to various stations. For the past two years he had been with an agency, and was devoting his time entirely to selling television programs to business concerns.

When he came to the Laboratory to take the work-samples, he had reached a crossroads and didn't know which way to turn. He had just refused the offer of a highly-paid television selling job and said he was so sick of selling he didn't think he could face another client. He was beginning to think something was drastically wrong with himself. He saw his problem at once when his aptitude results were explained to him. Because his background was in sales, he has set himself up as a sales consultant, planning sales and training programs for his clients. The subjective person fits well into consultant work, for people come to him for specialized advice and he doesn't have to go out and solicit business.

The Laboratory's files are filled with cases about unhappy subjectives who have tried to be salesmen. And often the HEL learns in unusual ways what has happened to persons tested. Only recently the wife of a man tested about four years ago brought their twelve-year-old daughter to the Chicago Laboratory to take the worksamples. The girl was bubbling over with excitement and told the test administrator that he wouldn't believe how the whole house had changed since her father had been tested. With the uninhibited frankness of the young, she said, "Daddy used to be so cranky it was awful, and now he's fun." She was excited because her father had just been elevated to a vice-presidential rank and was chief accountant in his firm. Before he was tested he had been selling. He proved to be extremely subjective with very high graphoria, low ideaphoria and fairly high vocabulary. At the Laboratory's suggestion that he had ideal aptitudes for accounting, he studied accounting in the evenings and achieved brilliant school success, which led to his present position. After the test administrator finished testing the daughter, he talked with the mother. She said that after three years in accounting her husband was earning far more than he ever did in twelve years in selling but, more important, he was infinitely happier.

When a salesman proves to have both extreme subjectivity and high structural visualization, readjustment can be exceedingly difficult if he has no scientific or engineering training to fall back on. One such man, tested in Boston, sold jewelry for a long-established firm. When he first started, he sold 220 per cent of his quota, the highest in the company. The second year he was third highest. The third year he quit. He is a tall, attractive man with a warm and pleasant smile, and it seemed strange to the human engineers that he should be unemployed. He said that he was disgusted with selling and wanted no part of it. There was, however, one aspect of his work that he had really enjoyed, and this was helping his clients set up their stores' displays—this uses structural visualization.

What had led to his quitting was that when he was three days late starting out on a sales trip, a new sales manager told him to get going. Instead, he resigned. He told the test administrator that he hadn't started out on the trip sooner because he was dissatisfied with the sales talk on a new line. He wanted to know more about it and get his talk in better shape before he approached his customers. This attitude is in keeping with the conscientiousness of the subjective person, but also, like most subjectives, he resented having a new boss and, most of all, being pushed. His most severe problem is that he has made so much money selling that he could not match it in any other field, especially since he has no specialty. He has a problem only he can solve. It is a difficult one and will take a sacrifice of both pride and money.

Another man tested who also proved to be subjective with high structural visualization had been working as a salesman and making good money. His wife reported that three years ago he had been so disagreeable to his family that he was almost impossible to live with until the Laboratory discovered his subjectivity and unused structural visualization. Knowing he was not a salesman, he then quit his selling job and took a mechanic's job in a factory at a beginner's salary. Now his wife says he is a changed person. He has progressed in his factory job to earning more money than in selling. But more important, he is happy as a mechanic.

Still another man with high structural visualization sold medical supplies but was restless and unhappy in his job. In two years of study, he acquired enough technical training to become an electronics specialist and, in keeping with his aptitudes, has started an electronics business of his own.

Very often persons who discover a sales aptitude from the tests change happily from other types of work to selling. A husband and wife did just that after being tested. He sold the retail business he had owned for twenty years and went into selling investments. His wife had worked for him as a bookkeeper and now sells real estate. He writes that both are happy and pleased about making the change and are doing well. "All this," says the letter, "is the result of things we learned about ourselves which gave us the courage to tackle new fields that fear would have prevented our trying otherwise."

A salesman with additional non-sales aptitudes is happiest selling in the fields which utilize these other aptitudes. Even if we have the perfect sales aptitude pattern and are successful in selling, our other unused aptitudes can make us restless and dissatisfied. What we sell must be meaningful to us if we are to get real satisfaction from selling. If our work employs our aptitudes, we are more likely to feel that satisfaction. If we are high vocabulary, we belong in a high vocabulary field where the persons with whom we deal speak the same language and the product or service we sell is something in which we believe.

Even if you think you want to be a salesman, if you lack the sales aptitudes and particularly if you are subjective, the human engineers from long experience caution against selling. But if you are the born salesman, selling can be fun and challenging if it holds the fresh interests and variety the highly creative, objective person needs and enjoys.

14

The Performing Arts

The performing arts add so much color and pleasure to our lives that it seems impossible to visualize life without them. Throughout history music, drama, the dance—all the arts—have mirrored the culture of the times among all peoples of the world. While at one time professional entertainment was enjoyed mainly by a privileged few, today almost everyone has access to it in one form or another. Television, radio, records, tapes, motion pictures, theater, and concerts bring the creative arts into our homes and communities, while easier travel enables many to go where they can enjoy the best of the entertainment world.

As everyone knows, the broad spectrum of entertainment ranges from low-brow to high-brow, from the cheap and vulgar to rare peaks of inspired artistry and beauty. It can appeal to our finer or to our baser instincts; it can enhance or erode the quality of life. And because the field is so diversified, it offers numerous opportunities for performers and their supporters not only to find self-expressive work but to help raise esthetic levels.

To most of us, performances by true artists are thrilling and even magical experiences that answer some need deep within us. Often entertainers interpret what we feel but cannot express ourselves. They may make us want to laugh or cry, to forget our own problems, or they make us more conscious of the problems of others; they may inspire us with deeper appreciation of true beauty and human life. Because the entertainment world is international, it broadens our knowledge of people and the world, providing a significant educational and unifying force.

As any acclaimed performer knows full well, there are no short cuts to lasting success. Talent alone does not make an outstanding performer. For most it is a long, slow climb with unrelenting practice to perfect skill. And while laying the groundwork often is a tedious and frequently discouraging process, the right aptitudes and skill-improvement are of equal importance.

Without exception, successful performers are extremely subjective. The general aptitude pattern includes also high ideaphoria and abstract visualization and, for top success, a high vocabulary. It is easy to see why subjectivity is essential. Performers are individualists who go their own way, who strive to build up an identity that sets them apart. The emphasis, calling attention to oneself, needs the subjective's natural tendency to self-dramatize. When he is in front of an audience he can lose himself in what he is doing in a way that is difficult, if not impossible, for the objective person who always is a little conscious of what others are thinking. But even more important is the fact that the objective person rarely wants to devote his time to so much solitary practice.

Although all performers need ideaphoria, it is especially important for actors. The flow of ideas enables them to imagine themselves as someone else, to give the original touches that mark the star. Theirs is a world of make-believe, of abstract ideas and concepts, and for this reason they need abstract visualization and not structural thinking ability. An actor also needs high vocabulary to give understanding, depth and fullness to a performance. And it goes without saying that along with inborn traits and vocabulary there must be a deep interest and feeling for one's field of entertainment, and a willingness to put in the hard work needed for success.

In the performing arts, as in any other kind of work,

those who achieve lasting success have high vocabulary. Those who lack it may have a brief flare of fame, perhaps in a novelty act that at the moment strikes the public fancy, but unless they have something special to offer, too often they sink into obscurity. As mentioned before, objective persons act more or less alike, but no two subjectives act alike. Each is unique. To stay successful, a performer needs a high vocabulary since he must find new ways to express his individuality to capture the public interest and must anticipate trends.

The human engineers have measured the aptitudes and vocabularies of many successful performers and have been amazed at their exceptionally high scores in English vocabulary. Even some of those stars who appear to have a low vocabulary in their performances, who may murder the English language or act the perfect fool or brassy loud-mouth, have a high vocabulary. They only are giving us what they think we want and are astute enough to ascertain these wants and to look ahead to future trends.

What high or low vocabulary can mean in the performing arts is shown vividly in the case of two actors who happened to be tested the same week in New York. About the same age, they had almost identical aptitudes. Both were extremely subjective with high ideaphoria, music and art aptitudes and abstract visualization; both were interested mainly in musical theatricals. But one was at the top in vocabulary and the other at the bottom. The high-vocabulary actor was starring at the time in a popular Broadway musical comedy; the low-vocabulary actor, who had shown great promise at the start of his career, was driving a taxicab.

But high vocabulary alone does not guarantee success, nor do talent and hard work. The medium for expression must fit the individual. One high-vocabulary actress had minor roles for years and never became a star until she was middle-aged and began playing eccentric character roles that suited her perfectly. Then she became world famous.

Music is such a significant part of the performing arts today that there probably are more opportunities for a musical career than ever before. Of the four measurable music aptitudes, tonal memory is the most important. This is your ear for music and you can't be any kind of a musician without it. This aptitude seems to be inherited for the Laboratory has found that children of musically-gifted parents invariably have the trait.

The professional performing musician is extremely subjective. As you may recall, the extremely subjective person does not fit comfortably or happily in the business world. Even when he is drawn into the business turmoil for a few years, he may later break down emotionally, or even mentally. When he has high tonal memory and ideaphoria, musical performance seems to be the answer for him. The human engineers advise young persons strong in these traits to regard music seriously as a career, selecting an instrument congruous with other aptitudes, or to think about singing or conducting. If structural visualization is present, composing should be considered, for this ability to think in three dimensions seems to enter into attaining musical structure in a composition.

Selecting the right musical career to utilize tonal memory is of first importance, not only from the standpoint of personal satisfaction and enjoyment, but for chances of success. The Laboratory has tested many persons who have everything they need for successful musical performance, including high general and musical vocabulary, yet never achieve the success they had hoped to attain. Often the reason is that they have chosen the wrong musical medium (composing, conducting, singing, playing) for aptitudes other than tonal memory enter the picture.

A great many of us begin with the piano, but unless we have graphoria and hand dexterities, despite strong tonal memory, we may get discouraged and give up the instrument, or if we persist never get very far. High graphoria is essential to play any instrument that has music written in more than one clef, such as the organ and piano. Without it, reading music is discouragingly slow, and even more so if you advance to the point where you encounter scores where notes look like bunches of grapes. When we lack hand dexterity, execution becomes impossibly laborious in contrast to what we hear mentally. The human engineers once believed that finger dexterity was the most important in playing the piano, but now believe that tweezer dexterity is the more essential. Conductors also need high graphoria for faster and easier reading of scores.

If we have low graphoria, we can play an instrument that has music written in one clef, or we can sing. And the other music aptitudes influence singing and the selection of an instrument. Pitch discrimination is necessary to play an instrument in which the pitch is not set, such as the violin. Singers, also, need much of this aptitude. To play such instruments as the trombone or trumpet we need timbre discrimination along with tonal memory. Persons high in timbre discrimination enjoy a musicial activity in which they control the quality of the sound. They like playing instruments which produce intense harmonics. Singers score the highest of all in timbre discrimination, using this control of sound wave form in placing their voices and in enunciation. There is some indication that actors and actresses also average high in timbre discrimination. The human engineers tell us that if we lack timbre but want to sing, we should join a chorus, choir or glee club. A well-known chorus conductor says that group singing demands a mediocre voice. This may be one that lacks timbre, for it is the overtones which color a voice. Men average higher in timbre discrimination than women.

Rhythmic ability is needed to play the drums, and probably enters into playing any music that rests heavily on meter or beat, such as rock and other dance music, marches and country music. Dancers, of course, need the aptitude. And for some reason or other, the human engineers are finding a high correlation between rhythmic ability and the ability to spell.

Besides taking aptitudes into account we need to select a musicial instrument which will afford us real self-expression. One very subjective housewife, who had scored exceptionally high in tonal memory, wrote me that she was worried about how to use it. "Of all musical instruments to have been trained in," she wrote, "the only one I know how to play and pour out my soul in is a trombone. I feel like a lonesome moose in some virgin wild." Having played the saxophone in the high school orchestra, I could sympathize and knew exactly how she felt. Feminine vanity can be a factor, for, outside of the flute, the facial contortions involved in playing most wind or reed instruments can be shattering to the ego of the woman who wants to look pretty, and may be the reason far more men than women play such instruments.

Those who become outstanding in music have a high vocabulary. Certainly successful conductors and composers have this ability. Among those tested by the Laboratory are two composers and one conductor who are known internationally. But although there undoubtedly are some musicians playing in bands, orchestras and groups who have a high vocabulary, musicians in general average low.

Perhaps a main reason low vocabulary is so predominant among musicians is that tonal memory is mature before the age of ten, long before structural visualization which matures at age twenty, before ideaphoria at twenty-three, and inductive reasoning at eighteen. This means that musicians really start their professional careers as much as ten years before others, before they have the chance to gain the general background indicated by vocabulary, and essential to later success. The musically-gifted youngster needs a very early start in building both general and musical knowledge to assure future success.

One young musician rose to the position of a highly paid orchestra leader and then, when he was forty-two, came to be tested to see why he had been fired after years in the same position. He had ideal aptitudes for conducting, but scored at the bottom 10 per cent in vocabulary. As he grew older he was expected to express more through his music than he could give. Audiences, who in large part are high vocabulary, expect an intangible musical quality which seems to go with high vocabulary, so that music needs more than aptitudes and technical perfection. For any performer to succeed, his vocabulary level must not be below the level of his audience.

Tonal memory is a very strong and basic aptitude and

when unused underlies much restlessness. Many of us have it without knowing so. But even if we do know, far too few of us think of it in terms of including it in our work. Yet sufficient outlet for it rarely is found in a hobby such as collecting records and listening to music. The Laboratory tests many persons highly gifted with music aptitudes who are reluctant to even consider a career in music. They feel it is too precarious. Others hesitate because they think they must become outstanding to justify it. Yet how many persons in other fields become outstanding? If the average musician went into other work he would not go far because of low vocabulary.

When an extremely subjective young person tests with exceptional tonal memory, structural visualization and ideaphoria, the human engineers urge him to consider composing seriously. We need more good composers. Yet trying to earn a living by composing is hazardous. The logical solution is to get a background in both science and music, so he can earn a living in some scientific field and try composing on the side. As pointed out earlier, our unused aptitudes seldom start demanding too much attention until we reach our late thirties when they start tormenting us, when they make us feel we aren't getting what we want out of life. Until then, our time has been filled by developing the aptitudes needed in our work. If we have also improved an aptitude we don't use in our work, we can find a way to make it a part of our life. One man who followed this path became an engineer, but also acquired a musical background and composed. When he was in his forties he wrote a hit popular song which brought him more money than he had made in all his years of engineering.

Although we may think of tonal memory's place in the performing arts as being limited to musical performance, composing and choreography, there are other areas where it is important. One is in photography, and certainly in movies and television there is opportunity. The human engineers are not certain just why tonal memory should be important to a photographer, but the most successful ones invariably score high in it.

One young man tested who was completely frustrated

in his management job proved to be extremely subjective with high tonal memory, structural visualization, ideaphoria, inductive and analytical reasoning, graphoria and foresight—certainly not a pattern for a contented executive, but one considered by the Laboratory as an ideal one for a successful photographer. The young man was advised to go into making films. Since photography already was his hobby, he said he liked the idea but it seemed so impossible and remote. He stayed on in his management job for a few years until he decided he could take it no longer, that perhaps he should take his aptitudes seriously. Several years later, the Laboratory heard from him. He had made the change, had worked harder than ever before, but was now making films successfully and enjoying the work thoroughly.

Apart from the entertainment world, music aptitudes seem to find use in unexpected places. Building construction men for some reason score high in tonal memory; successful surgeons usually have pitch discrimination, which seems to manifest itself in keenness of perception; persons who type from tapes need timbre discrimination. And just recently a prominent oil man telephoned the Laboratory to tell them that it was not giving sufficient emphasis to the use of musical aptitudes in work such as his own. He said he knew he was using his tonal memory and pitch discrimination, for he could sit in a truck, listen to drilling, and know by sounds exactly what was going on deep in the earth.

In any of the performing arts, there must be a supporting organization. The actor or actress must have a good play, and a playwright has subjectivity with high ideaphoria, abstract visualization, inductive and analytical reasoning and high vocabulary. Stage and costume designers are subjective with high ideaphoria, structural visualization, memory for design and hand dexterities. The executive and managerial jobs belong to the objective person. Directors have the group-influencing pattern of high ideaphoria, inductive reasoning and abstract visualization along with objectivity, and usually have memory for design and music aptitudes. But the producer is the straight executive with objectivity, high abstract visualization, low ideaphoria and high vocabulary, but often with both art and music talents. He needs this pattern to manage the affairs of highly creative groups of individualists, and to handle the financial and practical aspects of the business.

While there is much that is good, even superb in today's entertainment, many of us would agree that there is ample room for improvement. We should not ignore the importance of entertainment because many of us, especially young people, are influenced by television, radio and movies. Whether that influence is good or bad, whether it lifts or cheapens the quality of life, depends on those in the entertainment field. Tremendous power lies in their hands. Many parents complain of the dearth of movies to which they can bring their children; many want more good shows for youngsters on television. The entire field of performing arts offers a challenge to those whose aptitudes and interests lie in this area—an area that has become such an enjoyable and influential part of our daily living.

15

The Creative Arts

Since our earliest recorded history man has sought to express his ideas and emotions in some tangible form, whether it be through painting, sculpture, architecture or writing. The creative arts are a history of civilization, a visual evidence of the life and thinking of the times. The great works of art and literature have a quality that causes them to live, to be timeless, and to fill some deep need of the human spirit.

In the fine arts, the works of the masters reveal far more than perfect craftsmanship; there is an intangible quality that stems from the artist's deep sensibilities and close attunement to the pulse of life. It is this quality that distinguishes the masterpieces from lesser works of art and gives them immortality. Perhaps this quality is what the architect-painter Giorgio Vasari called "soul" in the sixteenth century. In writing of the life of Bramante, Vasari listed the qualifications of a great architect: "The architect must possess a soul, courage, genius, knowledge, and not only theory but experience and training to the highest degree."

Few of us have the talents of a great genius. But the creative urge is strong in many of us, and through following its dictates we can gain much inner satisfaction and often success. When we have high ideaphoria, this creative imagination must be used or it can destroy us through nervous tension and restlessness. This is especially true for the extremely subjective person with unused high ideaphoria who can too often create his own mental hell.

The Laboratory believes that extremely subjective persons with strong ideaphoria should seek some form of esthetic expression. If they have much inductive reasoning, they might write; if they have structural visualization, they might sculpt; if they lack both inductive reasoning and structural visualization, they might try painting. The painter also needs memory for design, observation and tweezer dexterity. Established artists tested by the Laboratory invariably score high in color perception.

Undoubtedly the true artist is extremely subjective. We have only to read the biographies of some of the masters to see how this trait is prominent. Their complete absorption in their art, their emotional intensity, their individualistic behavior, their determination to be themselves and express themselves in their own way and not imitate others, the long hours of working in solitude, all are characteristic of extreme subjectivity. The objective, artistically gifted person may have equal talent, but he rarely can force himself to put in the solitary effort and have the singleness of aim to become outstanding. However, the objective artist who disciplines himself to develop the needed craftsmanship and knowledge can be a very fine artist.

As any artist knows, the creative artist earns a precarious living. Often it takes years for an artist to find himself, to express what he wants to express, and to develop the needed techniques. Even then, much depends upon whether the times are ready for him, or if his work really merits recognition. Unless he has another means of support, he usually must compromise and commercialize his art ability, painting for himself in his free time. There are, of course, countless possibilities in commercial art in both public and private enterprises, in lay-out and illustration of books, pamphlets, magazines and the like.

One woman, a lay-out artist for a government agency, does her serious painting at home and has held at least three successful exhibitions at small but well-patronized art galleries. Other artists, who prefer to remain only in the fine arts, work in galleries and museums or teach while some, with inductive reasoning ability, write about art subjects. When the artist has structural visualization and perhaps proportion appraisal, he could work in anything from stage and costume design, window display, and industrial design, to interior decorating.

But another problem that confronts most high-creative subjective artists is the difficulty of conforming to business routine. They rebel at regimentation, at being restricted in any way. And most highly-creative people work spasmodically and for days may appear to do nothing, then suddenly begin to work like madmen. This way of working often is misunderstood by low-ideaphoria executives. They may not realize that for them to get the desired quality and originality, artists often must be allowed to work at their own speed and not be subjected to unreasonable deadlines and pressures.

The real happiness of the subjective person lies in creating his own individual life, not in following a conventional life style. Whether in fine or commercial art, the extremely subjective, highly creative artist undoubtedly belongs in the studio where he can express his ideas in his own way and on his own time. If he wants, he can work in the middle of the night and does not need to conform his working hours to a routine.

One highly successful commercial artist came to be tested when he had just quit his job in an advertising agency. He said he could not stand the pressure and restrictions and felt that the quality of his work suffered in trying to meet short deadlines. He decided to go into business for himself, where he first would create and then sell independently to different agencies. He now says he is far more content working this way. However, some commercial artists with less ideaphoria often enjoy being given ideas to execute, and get satisfaction from using their memory for design, tweezer dexterity and acquired skill.

Observation is another trait important to the artist. A

strange thing is that those without this aptitude believe they have it because they see and hear everything around them. But the person who is observant sees only one thing at a time; he sees it thoroughly until it becomes deeply impressed on his mind. The Laboratory has found that those who score high in the knowledge of paintings test invariably have high observation.

Abstract visualization ability is also a necessary artistic trait. Because they deal mainly with abstract concepts and one dimensional figures, most painters have abstract visualization rather than structural ability. Certainly this is apparent in the works of the Impressionists and in much of modern art. But sculptors, on the other hand, must have the ability to visualize solids clearly. Michelangelo, for example, must have had exceptionally strong structural visualization to create his masterpieces in sculpture and to give the three-dimensional quality to his paintings. But beyond this, his intense need to understand human anatomy, which drove him to furtive dissections of corpses at San Spirito, certainly points to strong structural visualization.

Proportion appraisal seems to be needed for package and product design. For some years the Laboratory believed that architects and artists needed this trait until further testing and research showed that instead they tend to score low in the test. It may be that the person who has the aptitude is one who follows precedents, for engineers, scientists and mechanics score high. The low-scoring person likes to work out a new way of attacking each problem, unhampered by preconceived concepts. Architecture represents a vivid example of this, where each problem demands an individual solution.

An architect tested recently, who lacked proportion appraisal, pointed out a difference between engineers and architects which may have bearing on this aptitude. "Engineers," he said, "think there are any number of possible ways to work out a problem, and that it doesn't matter much which you use; there is none of the refining of design, the search for the one perfect answer which characterizes the architect's office."

Of all the fine arts, architecture probably mirrors most vividly the social, economic and cultural progress of the times, and reflects human behavior and values. Architects who can give us the qualities that Vasari listed, who have "soul," who can combine the beautiful with the functional, are always needed. Perhaps the greatest challenge to architects today lies in our cities. We have become more and more urbanized and most of us respond to our environment. The architect who can create a beautiful city, or even one small spot of charm and beauty in a city, who can combine esthetics with the marvels of technology, performs an invaluable service.

In *The Conquest of Peru* William H. Prescott wrote: "The surest test of the civilization of a people—at least as sure as any—afforded by mechanical art is to be found in their architecture, which presents so noble a field for the display of the grand and the beautiful, and which, at the same time, is so intimately connected with the essential comforts of life."

Unlike artists and sculptors, successful architects are objective, but the sculptor-architect is subjective. The architect needs objectivity to work compatibly with others in the construction of his plans. He also needs structural visualization, high ideaphoria, memory for design, tweezer dexterity and graphoria. And the most successful ones tested by the Laboratory have a high vocabulary, and also make high scores in the vocabulary of architecture and knowledge of paintings tests.

Of all the creative arts, writing perhaps has had the greatest influence on our thinking and our deeds, and the written word has become one of our most valuable possessions. It is difficult to imagine a world without books or other forms of the written word. Ever since man began to think, individuals have struggled to record their thoughts. Even the Preacher in Ecclesiastes said, "Of making many books there is no end." From the various forms of the printed word we can gain knowledge, inspiration, entertainment, and emotional or spiritual satisfaction. What we read can color or give direction to our lives. The influence of writers is enormous. But whether that influence is good or bad depends not only on the writers themselves but on the judgment and integrity of their publishers.

A great many persons cherish a secret desire to write. On the surface it seems such an easy form of self-expression that many think anyone can do it if he wants to. But those who attempt it without the necessary aptitudes soon become discouraged. Yet aptitudes alone will not make a writer; plain hard work, self-discipline and a high vocabulary are essential ingredients.

The principal aptitudes of a writer are ideaphoria, inductive and analytical reasoning and abstract visualization. Graphoria is not essential but it does help in reducing errors in a manuscript. And without a doubt the best writers, and those who achieve greatness, are extremely subjective. The deeply introspective writer or one whose work requires extensive research, needs to be subjective. Writing is such solitary work that any writer who intends to make it his life work must be content to spend long hours alone with it.

If he had the aptitudes, the objective person can function as a writer but his outgoing nature rebels at too much isolation. This conflict between work and personality can result in his putting off doing the work as long as possible. As one writer said, there's always "that leaf on the lawn" he has to go out and pick up. For this reason, the procrastinator needs a fairly tight deadline or, if writing a book, needs to work under contract. He will do the work when he knows someone is expecting something from him.

With high ideaphoria, inductive reasoning and abstract visualization, the objective person is at heart a "group-influencer," and as such probably enjoys most writing about things he believes in and feels should be made known, rather than trying his hand at fiction. Often his subjects involve securing information from others, which uses his objectivity. In a writing job, he makes the best reporter, advertising writer, publicity person, and the like.

But any writer, whether subjective or objective, needs to believe in what he is writing about if his work is to be effective and, even more important, if he is going to be able to live with himself. Any serious writer probably would agree with John Ruskin's concept of why a book is written: "The author has something to say which he perceives to be true and useful, or helpfully beautiful. So far as he knows, no one has as yet said it; so far as he knows, no one else can say it. He is bound to say it, clearly and melodiously if he may; clearly, at all events."

For creative writing, high ideaphoria is essential. But for writing fiction or non-fiction, inductive reasoning is perhaps the most important of all the aptitudes, for it enables the writer to organize his presentation. The Laboratory believes that anyone who has strong inductive reasoning should write, even if he lacks ideaphoria. It is the aptitude of the professions, and in the professions published works increase success. Moreover, writing down thoughts and ideas helps to clarify thinking, important in any profession. When inductive reasoning is stronger than ideaphoria, the writer might become a scientific writer, historian, critic or essayist.

As any writer knows, writing is not a ready-made job, and each writer has to make his own place for himself. This is why the human engineers urge anyone with writing aptitudes who wants to write to start early in life to gain experience. One writer, tested years ago, who has since published one hundred and eight books, papers and articles, once wrote to Mr. O'Connor: "How wise you were to suggest, advise, encourage, instruct, inspire, cajole, inveigle, entice, stimulate, force, beat, kick, whip me into writing at the age of fourteen."

As with art, trying to earn a living by free-lance writing can be precarious unless one becomes an established author with a ready market for books or is a regular contributor to high-paying publications. Most writers, at least at the beginning, must hold some kind of paid job and relegate their personal writing to a hobby. Many hold writing jobs, and of course there are numerous opportunities in magazine and newspaper work, in advertising and public relations, and in radio and television. Government information offices use writers as do many non-profit organizations.

But a word of warning for the writer who takes a paid

writing job. The kind of writing we do must be in keeping with our interests, beliefs and vocabulary level or we can be miserable. The higher our vocabulary, the more selective we must be if we want to be able to live with ourselves. If we have aptitudes beyond the writer's pattern, we probably are most content working in the field of these aptitudes. For example, if we have artistic talent, we work more compatibly in related fields; if we have music talent, we belong in some sound or music field, and so on. Not only would we find more persons who share our interests, but we have the opportunity to use more of our aptitudes.

A writing job is not always the answer and in fact, can, be detrimental to the pursuit of serious writing and to developing one's own style. This may be especially true in writing projects where repetition abounds and work is judged apparently by weight rather than content. Some writers prefer jobs far removed from writing in order to approach their hobby without being influenced by the style used in their work.

Without editors, writers would be lost. The ideal editor is objective with high ideaphoria, and has inductive and analytical reasoning, abstract visualization, and a high vocabulary. In fact, editors average higher in vocabulary than writers. But the most essential trait of an editor probably is analytical reasoning, for he must see that the contents of a manuscript have unity and coherence. He needs objectivity to work compatibly with authors who usually are subjective. Also, a subjective editor may be inclined to want changes in a manuscript to coincide with his own concepts rather than with those of the author.

For success in any of the creative arts, vocabulary is of prime importance. The writer especially must have high vocabulary to give clarity and meaning to his works. The creative person who lacks knowledge also lacks the background he needs to express himself properly and to give to his creations that intangible something that sets them apart.

Apart from architecture, those who become outstanding in the creative arts invariably are extremely subjective. The objective person who loves art but doesn't want to create it himself can do much to help deserving artists gain a foothold. And those rich persons who spend fortunes buying the art of past masters could perform a great service by sponsoring young artists much in the manner of the Medicis. Who knows what great art might emerge under such sponsorship? Perhaps there could be another Renaissance.

There is every challenge in the world today for those in creative arts. It is in their power to bring more beauty, inspiration, quality and meaning into our lives and into that of future generations.

16

Changing Jobs

There seems to be something perverse in human nature that causes many of us to believe that pastures are greener on the other side of the fence. This is especially true when it comes to our jobs. We know the shortcomings and frustrations of where we are; the unknown holds promise of interest and glamor. Thus if we are in work that does not satisfy us, we may think if we move to a different employer, or even make a complete abrupt change in our type of work, our problems will be solved. Sometimes, by luck or careful planning, they may be. But unless we have the opportunity to use more of our aptitudes in the new job, too often after the newness and excitement have worn off we find the greener pastures only an illusion.

Many young persons starting their working career change jobs frequently, sometimes trying their hands at different kinds of work and often in different localities, which all adds up to experience. Many young men today, with their work plans interrupted or delayed by military service, have come back to civilian life with a broadened outlook and often a change of direction in mind. The great advantage of knowing our inborn abilities as early as possible is that we can orient ourselves toward a direction basically in keeping with our true talents and interests; and we can get the training needed to work toward our goal. And even though at first we may change employers in trying to find the organization where we feel we belong, we are spared much of the awful agony of floundering around to find where we fit best.

The Laboratory cautions of the dangers of making abrupt changes in our work. In nature itself, violent changes create chaos. Many who take the Laboratory's worksamples and find they are in work contrary to their aptitude pattern feel they should make the transition at once, that aptitudes alone would insure their immediate success. But skill and knowledge are of equal importance and these take time and effort to acquire. The better plan is to utilize our acquired knowledge and skill and endeavor to develop one additional aptitude at a time.

Very few of us are in the wrong work completely. Usually the trouble is that we lack knowledge and are using too few of our aptitudes. Although factors such as disagreement with company objectives, dim prospects for advancement, or incompatibility with co-workers enter the picture, a major contributor to restlessness and job dissatisfaction is unused aptitudes. You will remember that most of us test with eight or nine of the known aptitudes, but standard jobs rarely use more than three or four or often less. If we lack one aptitude for the job we hold, this is not so important; but if we lack three aptitudes basic to the work, the problem becomes far more serious and for any kind of job contentment adjustments must be made.

Actually, as mentioned before, up until about age thirty-five most of us are so busy developing a few aptitudes and trying to get ahead that our unused aptitudes may not demand so much attention. But what often happens is that, as we approach forty, we reach that moment of truth with ourselves and begin wondering if we are getting what we hoped from our life and work. At this stage many persons come to the Laboratory to take the tests, certain that change either to a completely different type of work, or to a new job with a different employer, will solve their problem.

Follow-up studies show that if we change employers at

this time of life, the chances are that we will move again within the next three years. Only recently, four men in their early forties, all high vocabulary, prosperous and in high positions, came to be tested because they were restless in their work. Each wanted to take a new job with a different organization; each told of the rare opportunities of the new situation and of the unendurable frustrations of the present.

Some years back, the human engineers would have advised them to go ahead, provided the new position paid more money immediately, carried a more exalted title, and would use additional aptitudes. But as a result of the follow-up studies, the Laboratory's position has changed. Mr. O'Connor said, "After the age of thirty-five or forty, do not shift to another employer no matter how alluring the prospects or how hampering the present. The chances of disappointment are staggering. Every man who comes to the Laboratory for advice honestly believes that both he and the concern he hopes to join are remarkable exceptions."

In a comparison of men who resign, presumably for greater scope, with those who continue in the same organization, it was found that the latter, despite annoyances, are better off than those who leave. In another study, involving twenty-eight individuals who changed employers with the assurance of more money and greater autonomy all but one moved again within three years. One moved six times in the next dozen years, with the result that his children suffered both grade loss and scholastic failure due to such frequent changes of schools.

Perhaps the major problem in changing employers after the age of forty is that we lose seniority; we can readily be eased out by a merger, let go by a new president with new policies, or dismissed if business falls off. The human engineers advise that rather than changing to an environment that probably is little different from the one we know, to analyze if what we plan to do in the new organization could be done where we are.

What we make of the job we hold and the job we hope to move up to depends so much upon our own initiative and our goals. It is possible to keep a job for which we have knowledge and experience, and by gradually adding aptitudes and specialized knowledge to ease our way into the work we want. And if we know what our real abilities are, if we are forced to work for a time in the wrong job, at least we understand why we feel as we do and can make allowances for it.

There are times when a seemingly insignificant change can make an enormous difference. There was a salesman in a large New York brokerage firm who never had sold much and was so discouraged he took the Laboratory's tests to see if he should make a complete change in his kind of work. He was positive he was extremely subjective. The tests showed him to have ideal aptitudes for his brokerage job—extreme objectivity, high graphoria, number memory, ideaphoria, abstract visualization and low inductive reasoning. The cause of his problem was a puzzle until he explained how he did his selling. He conducted almost all of his business over the telephone and rarely saw a customer in person. With his extreme objectivity and high ideaphoria, he needed to get out of the office and call on his customers. After he started doing this, his sales have more than tripled. But more important, he enjoys his work thoroughly.

Although any unused aptitude underlies restlessness and dissatisfaction with self, the ones that seem to create the worst problems at work are personality, structural visualization and ideaphoria. The extremely subjective person in an objective job, and the objective in purely subjective work can "lead lives of quiet desperation," for the work is contrary to their basic natures and adjustments must be made. The person with no outlet in his work for his strong structural visualization ability invariably experiences restlessness and frustration, and is the reason why so many high-structure, objective persons resign from big corporations as they approach forty.

The high-ideaphoria person in a routine job that makes no demands on his creativity is abnormally restless and unhappy. Often he develops nervous problems or takes to excessive drinking for escape. Or he may exercise his creativity by stirring up trouble, in imagining conditions which may not even exist, but which serve as a scapegoat for his restlessness and dissatisfaction. If we know what is causing our problems, we can at least try to do something about them.

A design engineer, unhappy working for a large corporation, came to the Los Angeles Laboratory to take the tests. He proved to be objective with very high structural visualization and ideaphoria. He had been doing purely subjective engineering work, and the human engineers suggested that he try to transfer to sales engineering, but in the meantime to start planning ahead for a business of his own. He made the move to sales engineering, which he enjoyed, but which also enabled him to make valuable connections useful to him in his future enterprise. After much careful groundwork, he resigned and went into business for himself. The undertaking has proved to be highly successful and, although he works harder than ever before, he says he is happier and more satisfied.

Many of us dream of a business of our own. We would like to be independent, to have the satisfaction of building something that is ours alone. Many who would like to be self-employed are afraid to try, feeling the risk is too great, and it is true that the mortality of small businesses is high. But the Laboratory is convinced that more of us who want to do it should do it, not only for personal but for practical reasons.

In business and industry especially, one never knows when his job might be in jeopardy—through a business decline, a reorganization, a merger, even the loss of a large contract. Nor can we know when we might be dismissed or demoted to make room for an outsider. Furthermore, most of us can expect to be retired at age sixty or sixty-five, sometimes earlier, and many do not want to end a career then, to mark time for the rest of their days. The Laboratory tells us that instead of shifting to another employer after the age of thirty-five or forty, to stay where we are and start developing gradually our own future enterprise. What we do should be based on our aptitudes, interests and goals as well as on our specialized skill and knowledge.

The old bromide, "Rome wasn't built in a day," is apt when it comes to starting one's own business. The Laboratory believes we need a good three months just to think about it and decide what it would be. Then, once the decision is made, we should devote time on weekends to planning and building what we have in mind. If we have high structural visualization, our plans should involve constructing something; if we are objective with high ideaphoria, our objective might be some type of selling, and so on. But several aptitudes may create problems. One is strong inductive reasoning, for persons strong in this aptitude often debate, argue, criticize, but postpone acting. They have trouble making up their minds and need to set time limits on themselves for reaching a positive decision. One such man, miserable in his job and eager to start his own business, was still unsettled as to his exact direction after eleven years of debating with himself about it. Yet the aptitude may be needed in starting a new enterprise, for new situations can arise that must be reasoned quickly and there is no past experience to fall back on.

The other problem can be low foresight, for persons low in this aptitude have difficulty sticking to an objective, in completing what they have started. Foresight may be essential in starting our own business, although the low-foresight person often needs only outside encouragement and urging to stay with a goal.

The HEL has some words of advice about starting a business: "Do not buy a business already encumbered with shackling policies, fixed ideas, and a set direction which even if patiently altered by the plenary powers of ownership, lie dormant. Carrying on another man's business does not give unhampered self-expression, and the satisfaction of creating from the beginning. Start with a clean slate, an invigorating establishment of your own, unhandicapped by the shadow of a former protagonist. To do this effectively, abandon all notion of shifting jobs. Achieving your own enterprise is not a week's effort, or a month's, but many years; and after the age of thirty-five can be started only by one who has steady work elsewhere which he does automatically after years of experience."

The Laboratory tests many young persons who express a hope of someday going into business for themselves. For those who really want to do so, the time to start planning ahead is now and not in some misty future. It may take five to ten years to establish a successful business and to even start one, we need knowledge and experience. One can't just jump into forming an enterprise. Then, too, we must lay our plans while holding down another job. Whatever we do, it should be not only in the field of our aptitudes, but on the level with our vocabulary.

Many start their own business in a partnership. But there are factors that can make or break a harmonious and successful relationship. Unless you are on similar vocabulary levels, you never will see eye-to-eye on many things. Also, unless your aptitudes complement each other, the results can be disastrous. It is a common tendency to think we double our strength if our partner is the same as we are, but it rarely can work out that way. For example, two executives with equal authority trying to run one business can be cataclysmic. Since many small businesses are based primarily on administration and selling, the ideal partner for the person with an executive aptitude pattern would be the sales type. Neither likes doing the work of the other, and they don't get in each other's way.

If we examine the most successful partnerships, we find the partners usually complement each other in aptitudes. An exception might be two extremely subjective persons who start a service organization of their own, such as two mechanics who open a small repair shop together. Each has his own work to do; if they are good mechanics, people come to them and they don't have to solicit business.

Some people who want to start a business dream of a little farm somewhere, visualizing an idyllic existence away from city and suburb. But in doing this, there are important factors to consider. First, specific knowledge of the type of farming planned is needed. Second, the real farmer needs to be subjective. The objective person can be a farmer only if he approaches farming at an executive level. Third, many farmers also need structural visualization because of the scientific aspects of the work, and because so many farm operations are mechanized. The other factor is vocabulary, and the high vocabulary person may be happiest if he settles in a community where he finds others similar to himself.

Despite the risks and hard work involved, there are numerous advantages in building your own enterprise. When intelligently planned and executed, self-employment is an opportunity to use your own aptitudes in your own way to suit your particular interests. Important, too, is the fact that you don't have to retire unless you want to. One man, now past the century mark, started his own business many years ago and still takes a very active part in it. He goes to his office for at least a part of every day, is bright and alert, and shows no signs of senility.

Those who would rather work for someone else—and this is true of most of us—need to plan ahead for what to do after retiring. All of us know retired persons who are unhappy and at loose ends, who after a long and busy working life no longer feel useful and yearn for something constructive to do. The waste of human resources, of talent, mature judgment and intelligence is appalling, but more important is what it does to the individual. The person who over the years develops an interest centered around his aptitudes and directed toward a goal, moves easily into retirement from a job to his own work.

No matter how we do it, or when, every change we make in our work should be an advance that brings us nearer to our goal, and at the same time offers the greater self-expression that comes from using our inborn aptitudes.

17

Problem People

In some fifty years of testing and research, the Laboratory has found that certain kinds of people have unusual problems in adjusting to life and work. Among them are those with so many aptitudes they are torn in all directions; the rare individual who has a vocabulary so high he is out of contact with his society; and the person whose eye dominance complicates his life. There are also those who avoid adjustment, who escape from reality in a euphoria induced by drugs or alcohol. The Laboratory has measured the aptitudes and vocabularies of all these types. Some they have helped greatly; with others they have failed. There are factors in life beyond the scope of our inborn traits that can contribute to adjustment problems. But when the problem relates to our work and the search for self-expression, the scientific measurement of aptitudes can pinpoint possible causes of the problem so that action can be taken to find solutions. The human engineers can only tell us what possible directions to take. The rest is up to us.

Many persons who take the worksamples strive hard to make high scores in all of them. In fact, some are indignant when they don't, and insist the tests must be at fault. What they may not realize is that having too many aptitudes creates a difficult problem, for no recognized occupation uses more than four or five of the basic aptitudes that make up a work pattern. The probability of success, which ought to increase with ability, actually decreases with more than five aptitudes.

The great problem the too-many-aptitude person faces is that there are so many directions in which he could go, yet none would use all of his aptitudes at the same time. He is inclined to switch from one kind of work to another as boredom with a job drives him to try something else. The best solution the Laboratory has found is for him to set his sights on solving a world problem, or build up unusual work on a broad scale that would enable him to use most of his aptitudes. For this, he needs both high vocabulary and specialized knowledge. With these, and hard work, he could become an outstanding person of his time. Without these, he can become an outstanding failure, little more than a jack-of-all-trades.

Unfortunately, about nine out of ten of the many-aptitude persons tested are low vocabulary. The reason often can be traced back to school days, for with many aptitudes they can get by without making an effort to actually acquire much knowledge. Very often, if they go to college, they flunk out.

Some years ago, a forty-two-year-old man tested in New York was a striking example of what too many aptitudes and low vocabulary can mean. At the time he was working nights in a garage, parking and washing cars. He told the test administrator that he had been unable to finish high school because of the need to help support his family. His first job was clerk in a grocery store. Anxious to do better, he had studied accounting and worked up to become comptroller of a textile company. This job lasted for a time and then he had moved to become assistant production manager of a mill. When this did not satisfy him, he had decided to go into selling where he did quite well but this was interrupted by having to serve in the Army.

Returning to civilian life, he decided to use his G.I. Bill to study crooning, for he thought now that he would like to become a singer of popular songs. He soon gave up singing and returned to selling. Then he went into the selling business for himself but after six months he took the night garage job. He told the human engineers, "I get bored with every job I take. It is alright for just so long, and then I get fed up with it and want to do something else."

He scored high in every aptitude, but at the very bottom in vocabulary. It is the old story: the brilliantly gifted young man of promise, for whom the promise does not come true, his outstanding capacity not honed by knowledge and not channeled toward a goal.

For all of us, vocabulary is essential, but for the many-aptitude person it is vital. Without it, he often becomes the drifter, romantic perhaps in song and story, but not in real life. One cannot even begin to think of solving broad problems without the tools for thinking. The Laboratory has found that it is useless to convey the concept of a broad, problem-solving goal to the low-vocabulary, many-aptitude person, and urges vocabulary building as a first step before any career choice can be made. Often it has difficulty persuading young persons of the importance of increasing vocabulary. Perhaps it is as Lord Chesterfield said, "Young men are apt to think themselves wise enough, as drunken men are to think themselves sober enough."

But even when they have a high vocabulary, the many-aptitude person is not always easy to convince that a standard occupation is rarely the solution to his problem. One trouble is not merely too many aptitudes, but their inconsistencies. The subjective person with structural visualization revels naturally in structural puzzles, but objectivity and structural visualization pull in opposite directions, toward people and toward things. Ideaphoria and graphoria are restless companions, the first a wild flow of ideas, the second rigidly controlled precision. Every unused aptitude causes restlessness and a dissatisfaction with our own accomplishment. Since no standard job uses all his gifts, the many-aptitude person in a sense must create his own job.

As mentioned previously, one method that seems to work is thinking in terms of a problem of true interest, then getting the specialized training and knowledge needed to work towards its solution. One objective man with many aptitudes, greatly interested in food production, secured agricultural training and is tackling the problem of feeding the world. City planning seems to offer a satisfactory outlet for the many-aptitude person, as does management of a small city. Still others work at standard jobs but find outlet for their other aptitudes in a variety of avocations. For some this suffices, but the many-aptitude person who can pool his talents in a single endeavor directed at solving a world problem has the unique opportunity of making a lasting contribution to the world.

While a high vocabulary is necessary for achieving worldly success and for bolstering our inner resources and self-confidence, occasionally the human engineers encounter a person so high in vocabulary there is no place where he can fit. He is not in real contact with this world. His trouble seems to be that he doesn't lack for words, but is inclined to be almost in the stratosphere, compared to most of us, and can't get down to earth. He rarely can find anyone who speaks his language. The average high-vocabulary person uses simple language, but the too-high-vocabulary person is inclined to use terms peculiar to his own way of thought. Usually he becomes impatient with others not so proficient in word-knowledge. Frequently he drops out of college. If he gets a job, he soon quits, for he can't communicate with his fellow-workers, including those at the top. A possible solution to the problem may be to work in a unique high-vocabulary field in which he can move up quickly, or to start some high-level enterprise of his own. Two of the highest vocabulary persons ever tested by the Laboratory have become severe alcoholics.

Eye dominance may or may not create problems for its possessor. About one in four of us score left-eyed in the Laboratory's eye dominance test, and because of inherent left-sidedness should be left-handed. But the world is designed for right-handed persons and all too often the left-eyed person is brought up to use his right hand. The resulting unnatural strain seems to underlie excessive nervousness and unusual clumsiness. Often such a person has a high degree of nervous energy and drive. But more serious consequences often occur—speech defects, laborious reading, and the like. The person who tests right-eyed and left-handed may have similar problems.

The Laboratory believes that we should use the hand that coincides with the dominant eye; that is, if left-eyed, we should be left-handed, and vice versa. Many persons in whom this crossed dominance has been detected by the Laboratory have decreased nervous tension, cured speech problems and lessened reading difficulties by gradually learning to use the proper hand. But the transition must be extremely gradual; a too-rapid changeover greatly exaggerates the symptoms. Even though crossed dominance may give its possessor little trouble at the moment, the Laboratory urges switching gradually to the proper hand, for the unnatural tension induced can take its toll in later years.

Perhaps one of the most serious problems today is the widespread use of drugs among youth. It may be true that many of the young who experiment with drugs do so because they think it the accepted thing to do, but those who continue drug use usually are seeking escape from inner tension and feelings of inferiority. The human engineers are measuring the aptitudes of more and more young drug-users, and a pattern is emerging that seems more than just coincidence. Almost all users show strong structural visualization that is not being used in any way.

Although every unused aptitude generates problems, structural visualization more than any other aptitude causes school troubles and foments restlessness. Yet it is not until the last years of high school that there is any real opportunity for the structurally-minded youth to use the aptitude in his school work. Biology courses may tax structural visualization, but too often they are lecture courses. The structurally-minded boy (or girl) must endure years of schooling before he can find outlet for this trait. And because he has the aptitude, he lacks the abstract visualization needed to savor history, literature, languages, and even reading. He feels instinctively that he has ability, but there is little in which he can achieve recognition. He needs gratifying success, which he doesn't get in school.

Since schools do not challenge structural visualization, the parents must give such children an early start in developing structural outlets that can be continued through school, college, and in later life. It is important to remember that the trait is useful not just in mechanics, carpentry, masonry, scientific hobbies and the like, but is a problem-solving aptitude that can be satisfied by investigating any unexplained question.

As we have already noticed structural visualization is different from the other known aptitudes in that it is not transmitted from father to son. A son inherits the ability from his mother, a daughter from either parent. The other aptitudes are inherited also from either parent. A non-structural father may have difficulty understanding a structurally-minded son, and may discourage rather than promote structural interests, so that they may have problems finding a common ground of interest. The same situation may arise in a mother-daughter relationship when a mother lacks the structural visualization which her daughter has and they have difficulty achieving a closeness. Few such problems would exist if parents would recognize the need for the structurally-gifted to find an absorbing outlet for the trait, and be encouraged and helped to do so.

While it is true that close family relationships result from mutual interest and encouragement of individual talents, it is especially crucial with structural visualization since it is the one aptitude unused in school work during so many of the formative years. The subjective youngster with the aptitude, if allowed to go his individualistic way, usually is drawn naturally to structural hobbies. The objective, on the other hand, is drawn to both people and things, and may need extra stimulation in finding a structural outlet to exercise his mind, for with the aptitude unused he merely uses hours, not his mind. This disuse, coupled with the restlessness caused by not using the structural visualization aptitude and the unhappiness of having a talent unrecognized both at school and at home, may be a significant aspect of the drug situation. Drugs ease tension and pass hours without using the mind.

A young college student tested recently had admitted freely that he was on drugs, and said he wanted to break away but just couldn't seem to do it. He tested objective with very strong structural visualization which he never had used. He was advised that if he wanted to give up the habit he must use his structural visualization and perhaps get a job as a mechanic. The young man took his advice and although it was far from easy for him, through intensive use of his structural visualization, he has quit drugs completely. Another young college student, on drugs and with the same aptitudes, changed from liberal arts to architecture where he could use structure, and is now off drugs.

There is yet another factor that may be of real significance with regard to high structural visualization and drug use. This is the lack of abstract visualization and many young persons today are concerned mainly with abstract concepts which the high structure youth has difficulty grasping and feels set apart. But through drugs he can move into their abstract world. One young man, high in structural visualization and once on drugs but now off them, told me he was certain this was why he took drugs.

There is little doubt that the alcoholic, too, drinks to relieve some unbearably strong inner tension. What causes the tension is an individual problem. When the tension springs from maladjustment in work and goals in life, self-knowledge through the scientific measurement of his aptitudes, and subsequent clarification of possible causes of his problem, may help him. The Laboratory has tested alcoholics who, through adjusting their work, have stopped drinking; it has tested others who have not. The Laboratory can only point out some of the causes of tension that may or may not lead to alcoholism, and the rest is up to the individual.

Many of the alcoholics tested by the Laboratory have been highly gifted rather than deficient in talents. In fact, two of the most brilliantly gifted persons the Laboratory has ever tested were alcoholics, plagued by a lack of goal and expression of their abilities.

Entirely unsuitable work may lead to alcoholism, for unusual tension builds up from trying to be what we are not. One severe alcoholic, working as a salesman, tested extremely subjective with high ideaphoria and music aptitudes. He never had used his music. He took up musical study, became a performer—and has stopped drinking.

In fact, the misplaced, extremely subjective person may be the most frequent alcoholic. The right work for our personality is essential for personal contentment and self-expression. While the objective person doing subjective work may be unhappy, he is not so tortured as is the extremely subjective in purely objective work who by nature is sensitive, introspective and retiring. Trying to behave objectively causes excessive tension when continued over a period of time.

The high-vocabulary person working with low-vocabulary people may be another who becomes an alcoholic. The human engineers have found that such a person, no matter how objective, invariably thinks he is subjective. Because he can't find a common ground with his fellow-workers, he feels he is at fault and tries desperately to conform, to feel he is one of them. Yet the others instinctively recognize his difference and act accordingly, which only serves to increase his feelings of uniqueness and subjectivity. If, in addition, he has no chance to use his strong aptitudes, his predicament is even worse and excessive drinking may be the result. One such man, who did not even know he had a high vocabulary, was working as a bell-hop when tested, spending almost every cent he made on liquor. When he learned he had not only vocabulary but all the aptitudes of a successful journalist, he stopped drinking, went back to school to study journalism, and is now a reporter.

Ideaphoria at loose ends could well underlie many cases of alcoholism. As mentioned before, it must be guided by another aptitude and directed toward some goal or it results only in overpowering restlessness and nervous tension. The alcoholic housewife could well be lacking creative outlet for her high ideaphoria.

All of us have problems; all of us go through various

periods of adjustment. But problems and adjustments are such that some people often need outside encouragement, help and understanding. A great advantage of knowing aptitudes and their influence on human behavior lies not only in self-knowledge, but in giving us a deeper understanding of others.

18

Marriage and the Family

If there is one place we should be able to really be ourselves, to find love, peace and friendship, it is at home. Samuel Pepys probably expressed the feeling of most of us when he wrote, "I do hate to be unquiet at home." And it was Friedrich Nietzsche who observed wisely that "it is not lack of love but lack of friendship that makes unhappy marriages." True friendship stems from mutual understanding and respect, from the acceptance of the other person for what he is and not what we think he should be. An important by-product of the Laboratory's research and measurement of inborn traits is a deeper understanding between husbands and wives and between them and their children. Our natural abilities are an integral part of us, and as such affect our lives at home as well as at work.

In 1922 when the Laboratory started its research in a factory, marital happiness probably was the last thing it thought of as having any connection with its studies. Yet over the years a great many husbands and wives have taken the tests to find out their career aptitudes and then have discovered a new understanding of each other. Many tell how knowing their own and each other's aptitudes has cleared up a variety of misunderstandings and drawn them closer together. So many of us expect the other person to be as we are, to think the way we do, to do things the way we do them, and too often we criticize and find fault if they don't.

In most marriages, it rarely is the big matters that cause friction; more often it is the little annoyances that irritate day after day, until they build up to form big dissensions and barriers that may lead to separation or divorce. Plutarch may have recognized this when he wrote: "A Roman divorced from his wife, being highly blamed by his friends, who demanded, 'Was she not chaste? Was she not fair? Was she not fruitful?' holding out his shoe, asked them whether it was not new and well made. 'Yet,' added he, 'none of you can tell where it pinches me.'"

One young couple tested found that finger dexterity, of all things, provided a clue to an antagonism growing between them that was assuming serious proportions, almost to a point where separation was being considered. What had happened was that the wife's clumsiness in handling things grated on her husband's nerves. She was always breaking dishes, chipping glasses, making a noisy clatter with dropped pots and pans; she couldn't screw the toothpaste cap on straight. He couldn't understand it and would become so irritated he would accuse her of being sloppy. Not only would this upset her so much that she would become more of a butter-fingers, but it would put her on the defensive. To retaliate, she would pick at his faults, real or imaginary, which normally she would have disregarded, and quarrels became more and more frequent. When they found from the tests that he scored a rare 100 per cent in finger dexterity and she had none at all, it dawned on both of them that this difference was a major cause of their dissension, and the air has cleared considerably. They laugh about it now.

Some years ago the Laboratory, out of curiosity, plotted the aptitude scores of four hundred married couples who had taken the tests in the past. It wanted to see if, from an aptitude standpoint, we marry our opposites or choose duplicates of ourselves. Apparently as far as personality and the other aptitudes are concerned, we marry anybody. Only one aptitude showed any suggestion that we might choose a mate like ourselves and this was finger dexterity. Men who scored high in inductive reasoning tended to choose wives with the aptitude, but high-scoring women chose those who were either high or low in it.

The strongest correlation turned out to be in vocabulary scores, which gave some indication that we tend to choose mates with similar knowledge levels. And there were some geographical differences. Women in the Southwest averaged higher in vocabulary than their husbands, while men in the eastern part of the country averaged higher than their wives.

Actually, a similarity in vocabulary may be of more importance to a happy and successful marriage than many of us realize. Husbands and wives on near vocabulary levels are more likely to understand each other, to speak the same language, and be able to really talk to each other. If the vocabulary gap between them is too wide, they may have difficulty finding a common ground and each tries to pull the other up or down to his or her level, which may lead to conflict.

While our aptitudes may not have bearing on whom we marry, a knowledge of our own and those of our mate can shed light on various sources of contention, some seemingly minor but others of serious importance. One problem that arises frequently in many homes is trying to get the husband to repair things around the house. For some reason, many women think just because a man is a man he can be a mechanic, plumber, electrician, carpenter, in general a do-it-yourselfer, and enjoy doing it. If he has structural visualization, or perhaps even proportion appraisal, this can be true. But if he lacks structural ability particularly, trying to get him to do these things can be a lost cause and nagging about it only makes matters worse. Not only is he instinctively unsure of himself in attempting such work, but he has little inclination to try. When one wife saw from the tests that her husband lacked structural visualization, she exclaimed, "Now I see why it would take an Act of Congress to make my husband fix anything in the house. I always accused him of being stubborn and lazy!"

Another wife had resented the fact that her husband spent so much time in his basement workshop, or fussing with the motor of the car. She thought he did it to get away from her until the tests showed him to be extremely subjective with high structural visualization. But the subjectivity cleared up another point that had bothered her, and this was his frequent reluctance to attend social affairs. She was beginning to think he didn't want to be seen with her. He, on the other hand, saw that because of her objectivity and high ideaphoria she needed more social life, so they have compromised on their activities.

Sometimes the situation is reversed and an extremely objective husband with a subjective wife may not understand why she doesn't enjoy social life as much as he does, especially large gatherings where she must meet and talk with strangers. This can create complications, for many extremely objective men are in sales or politics and attendance at a variety of social functions often is obligatory, a part of their job, and their wives are expected to be there. A grasp of the difference between subjective and objective personalities can help such couples reach some degree of understanding and compromise.

When personality opposites marry, it is essential that the basic nature of each be understood and appreciated, not only for peace and friendship at home, but in relation to work. A too common situation is that of a wife with executive aptitudes who tries to push her subjective husband into administrative work. Because executive ability comes naturally to her, she may think everyone should have it. But when her pep talks for more money, more drive, greater aggressiveness, and a more impressive show of executive ability fall on deaf ears, she may think her husband lacks spunk and ambition. By trying to nag him into action, she feels she is helping him, but the opposite is true. Such husbands may agree with Proverbs: "It is better to dwell in the corner of the housetop, than with a contentious woman in a wide home." One scientist, because his executive-type wife insisted, gave up research to become an unhappy and mediocre business executive. The human engineers are certain that this man had the potentialities of a truly great scientist.

A young minister and his wife were happily married,

but the wife's dwelling on his lack of executive ability was a sore point between them. She sincerely believed that she was helping him by urging him to be more business-like. She knew he was an outstanding minister, and that his inspiring sermons were attracting increasing numbers to church attendance and membership. So she kept telling him if only he would develop executive qualities, he could go far in the Church. When they took the tests, she was surprised to learn that she was the executive in the family, but she realized why she was trying to make him be one. She saw, also, that the subjectivity and creative and reasoning abilities that made her husband so excellent in the pulpit were not executive traits. She is now handling as many executive matters for him as she can.

To be ourselves and to get satisfaction from life, we need to use our natural abilities, preferably with some goal in mind. The housewife who is a born executive needs an outlet. Executive ability enters into operating a smooth-running household, but when it spills over into managing the lives of her husband and children, the results are certain to be unhappy. The author firmly believes that few, if any, marriages can be successful unless the husband is the head of the home. The executive wife needs to find outlets for her managerial abilities beyond the running of her home. It need not be a regular job unless she wishes it, for there are so many worthwhile volunteer activities where she can put her talents to constructive use, and at the same time get the self-expression she needs.

No matter what her aptitudes are, almost any woman at home needs to develop some activity based on her talents and interests that is hers alone, that offers self-expression, and gives her a feeling of achievement in her own right. It need not interfere in any way with marriage, family, and home life if she plans her time intelligently. Usually it serves to make her more interesting in the eyes of the family and enhances home life, particularly if her husband understands her aptitudes and encourages their development.

Foresighted women can avoid the pitfalls of future restlessness and feelings of uselessness so many experience when children leave home, if they begin early to develop a life interest of their own. If vocabulary and specialized knowledge have been built up along with her avocation, when she wants or needs to get a job, she has something to offer. The human engineers see the problem almost daily of middle-aged housewives who don't know what to do with themselves. And while it is possible for a woman to build up an interesting life for herself at almost any age, the problem is far simpler if she begins early to develop her talents. And knowledge, developed talents and interests help to bolster inner resources, so essential to keep us from turning bitter as we grow older and are so often left alone. It was a nun who wrote, "A sour old woman is one of the crowning works of the devil."

While knowledge of their inborn traits can deepen understanding between husband and wife, knowing their children's strong points and shortcomings offers valuable guideposts in their upbringing, and can contribute much to achieving a close and happy family relationship. The so-called generation gap can be narrowed considerably when parents understand their children's natural abilities and interests and give help and encouragement in developing them.

All of the known aptitudes can be measured in children when they are between the ages of nine and eleven. Even at age nine we can learn if our child is objective or subjective, if he is structurally minded, if he is high or low graphoria, if he has crossed dominance of hand and eye, and if his vocabulary is progressing as it should. In the next two years, the other aptitudes have matured enough to be measured, and we can know if he has art or musical talent, if he has ideaphoria and thus needs ample creative pursuits, if he has an ability for learning languages, and so on. We can learn if he has too many aptitudes; we can know again where he stands in vocabulary. All these have a direct bearing on his future happiness and adjustment in life.

Both vocabulary and graphoria are important factors in college selection. The Laboratory believes that the high-graphoria student is best placed in a large school where he gets the competition he needs. It believes that the high-vocabulary young person belongs in the older institutions, partly because of extensive library facilities, but mainly because he has more opportunity to find others, including his instructors, like himself. The low-vocabulary student stands a far greater chance of success in the newer, less conditioned schools, and in small schools and colleges where he can receive more individual attention.

As pointed out previously, knowing if a child has structural visualization is especially important since he has no opportunity to use it during so many of his school years, and outlets for it must be found at home. He often has school problems, due mainly to his disinterest in abstract subjects and restlessness induced by unused structural visualization. All young people need something from which they can gain self-confidence and incentive. Because the structurally-minded youngster is more interested in things than ideas, he usually needs help in building vocabulary, the lack of which can add to his school problems. A library built around his particular structural interests, visits to places that relate to them, meeting and talking with those in the field are all ways that parents can help to build his vocabulary, and at the same time help to bolster a confidence and ambition that can carry over into his school work. The importance of these outside outlets for structural visualization is too vital to be ignored. And when we consider the possible relation of unused structural visualization to the current drug problem, it becomes of even more serious concern.

When we know the aptitudes of our children, we can see them as individuals and not just as replicas of ourselves. We can see inherited family characteristics come to light and recognize them for what they are. Yet each child has his own combination of inborn traits that affect his behavior, his interests, and his dreams and ambitions. When we realize this, we are better equipped to give appropriate guidance to the child. Perhaps the greatest advantage of knowing a child's real abilities is that they point to the directions in which to go, and help him avoid mistakes that can affect his life. This awareness of the field of work suited to his particular combination of aptitudes, of knowing where he stands the best chance to find success and self-expression, enables him to set a goal and choose the education he needs to follow his dream.

This sense of direction, of knowing what you are and where you want to go in life, is more essential for young people today than it probably ever has been. Many in high school and college are confused about their role in a chaotic world they would like to see changed. So many children have so much to offer if only they could choose a direction right for themselves. But in college many are drifting aimlessly; others are groping to find themselves. The human engineers test many of these young persons who are plagued by career decisions, or dissatisfied with their college work. Too often they are heading in directions contrary to their aptitudes, or are in schools wrong for their particular needs and vocabulary rating.

School counselors provide many valuable services, but we can't expect our schools to raise our children for us. This is the job of parents. Nor can we expect the Laboratory to do it. It can measure inborn traits and vocabulary, interpret their meaning, help pick general directions in which to go and reveal those to avoid, but the rest is up to parents and to the individual. And what more logical place to find this knowledge useful than in our most important and closest relationship, in understanding better our children and the person with whom we choose to spend our life?

19

Philosophy and Goals

The basic goal of the Laboratory is to uncover and measure our inborn traits so that we can know ourselves better and find the work we do best, but in so doing have a greater chance for achievement, for leading a fuller, more meaningful life, and for gaining a feeling of rightness and naturalness within ourselves. But the broad goals lie deeper, for it is only through greater human understanding that we can hope to put an end to many of our man-made troubles, to wars, injustices, and "man's inhumanity to man."

Just as the development of physics and chemistry opened the way to material progress, human engineering is charting new paths to human understanding by applying the experimental method of the exact sciences to the study of humans. It is by this means that the Laboratory hopes to arrive at a sound approach to human understanding based on fact, reason, and calculation, rather than on emotion and imagination.

Mr. O'Connor expressed the following views: "I have seen the telephone appear and spread its voice; the automobile come into being; airplanes leave the ground and cross the ocean. Unbelievable mechanical progress and with all this there is still much man-made misery, human injustice, tragic dissatisfaction with life.

"The science of physics, chemistry, astronomy and mathematics has accomplished marvels. The Human Engineering Laboratory began with the idea that it might be possible to apply the approach of the exact sciences, particularly of chemistry, to an understanding of human behavior and, as a result, increase human happiness, lessen mental misery, reduce nervous breakdowns.

"For nearly fifty years the Laboratory has followed unceasingly this precept. First it has made measurements, such as are the basis of all exact sciences. Then the Laboratory has tried to determine and improve the accuracy of these measurements, much as chemistry has improved the accuracy of its analyses.

"So much of science has been applied to war, that many of the younger generation are avoiding it. Some suggest stopping all technology until mankind catches up. But man has thought seriously, and talked and written about himself for 5,000 years. Progress in human understanding must go faster. Applying the technology of the exact sciences to an understanding of man is at least one approach."

Human engineering itself has followed roughly the history of chemistry. For some 2,000 years, chemists spoke of earth, fire, air, and water as elements, and which did nothing at all to open scientific doors. It is hard to realize that it was only several centuries ago that chemists began to think of chemical elements in such terms as oxygen and hydrogen, but it was then that they began the laborious isolation of the chemical elements.

In a similar fashion, so have such human traits as concentration, motivation, and application been talked about for years, but have not led to a better understanding of people and their behavior. In its pioneering, the Laboratory began with the idea that it might be possible to isolate mental elements, genetic traits, much as chemists had isolated the chemical ones. And just as in chemistry, where an element is considered to be one if it cannot be broken down further, the human engineers consider an aptitude a true one if it cannot be broken down, if it refuses to correlate with any other aptitude. As we have seen, nineteen of these mental elements have been isolated, paralleling in many ways the isolation of the first nineteen in chemistry, and proving without a doubt that it is possible to isolate mental traits.

The next great step in chemistry came in 1817, with the recognition of a periodic arrangement of the elements, the *periodic table*, which is, of course, the basis for the present understanding of atomic structure. At that time, only about thirty-five elements were known, yet this orderly arrangement was a tremendous step ahead. Not only did it give scientists some idea of how many elements there were, but there were gaps in the table that provided clues for the discovery of new ones. Some of the elements did not fit in, showing scientists that they were not elements after all.

Similarly, the next great goal of the Laboratory is something similar to a periodic table of mental elements, possibly when about fifteen more aptitudes have been isolated. With such a periodic arrangement, it would be possible to get some idea of how many mental elements there are and where to look for new ones and, at the same time, perhaps eliminate some now known.

The human engineers are certain that there are many more aptitudes yet to be discovered. For example, they would like to be able to isolate and measure such traits as a sense of humor, intellectual curiosity, judgment, taste, and others that some of us have and others don't, but which help make up our character.

But just as a chemical analysis does not make a new chemical, neither does analysis of a mental trait make an aptitude. There is a long way between analysis and result, but the analysis serves as a basis for action. And research is long, slow, and expensive. No matter how much time, effort and money have gone into trying to isolate an aptitude, if it is found that it does not add to human understanding it is discarded. Standards of the Laboratory in research as important and difficult as this, must be kept as high as human frailty allows.

If we humans could be analyzed as chemicals are, the process would be far simpler. But we humans are complex; we have emotional and spiritual needs; we have minds with which to think. The individual whom the Laboratory tests gets an inventory of his inborn traits, an explanation of what they mean, and possible directions to take—factual data about himself on which to build a program toward self-expression and a richer life. And just as the research chemist turns over the new knowledge for others to use, the human engineers turn over its knowledge to the individual to use in working out his own salvation, for he alone knows what he wants to do with his life.

It is for this reason that the Laboratory uses only the professional individual approach in all its testing. After all, our aptitudes are a part of ourselves, and as such are personal and private; they are not public property. And although the Laboratory gets numerous appeals to do mass testing, it intends to continue using only this individual approach designed to help each person find himself or be himself, while at the same time to be assured that all information about himself is kept strictly confidential. Because all Laboratory records are confidential no names of persons tested are revealed. The temptation to publicize is great, for included among the individuals tested would be some of the best-known names in the country.

Recently a prominent army officer took the Laboratory's tests eager to learn his weaknesses so he could build up a strong staff to supplement them. He knew that all findings would be confidential, and that his weaknesses would not be broadcast throughout the world.

Along with maintaining its professional individual approach, another goal of the Laboratory is to establish more branches in more areas than it now serves, not only to make the services available to more persons, but to get a greater cross section of individuals for research purposes. But because the Laboratory is a non-profit scientific and educational research organization, and income dependent almost entirely on testing fees, expansion of facilities has been slowed down for financial reasons. The Laboratory has been fortunate, however, in receiving support from individuals and private institutions who realize the vital need for furthering the work.

Johnson O'Connor was asked what were some of the more distant goals of the Laboratory. One is to learn more about subjective personality and to publicize the results obtained. "I am convinced," he said, "that half, perhaps more, of the inmates of our mental hospitals were originally normal subjective individualists living in an objective world. Subjective persons start as members of a minority group, and so in a sense abnormal, different from the majority. Persons caught doing something 'queer' are committed for observation to a psychopathic institution, and twenty-four hours in this atmosphere may turn many of these subjective individualists permanently mad. But testing inmates of mental hospitals is not the answer. It is then too late. We must do everything in our power to give those who score subjective an understanding of themselves."

He was also asked about crime, and what greater human understanding could accomplish there. He replied, "We need to know if honesty is acquired or inherent, if it can be taught. With a bit more understanding of human beings we certainly could reduce crime. Those few so-called 'criminals' whom we have tested, and they are very few, were analyzed as trying to find an outlet for their idle aptitudes which they then applied to their criminal activities. We must urge every individual who comes to us to use all their aptitudes and not leave some idle."

With a better understanding of human beings and their behavior, and by raising vocabulary levels, it should be possible to bring needed improvements to government, to education, to working environments, and to relationships among peoples of the world.

The author's husband expressed a thought that bears repeating. In essence he said that because our true aptitudes are born with us, they must be gifts from God, given to us in love and with free will to be used as we see fit. And as with any precious gift that is given to us by someone who loves us and we love, we should treasure it, take care of it, use it, and not throw it away or keep it hidden. But because these gifts are given in love, should they not also be used in love, in helping to make the world a better place?

Human engineering started boldly and courageously some fifty years ago with the simple goal of trying to get the right man in the right job. Over the years, guided by the inspiring genius of Johnson O'Connor, the human engineers have proved that our mental traits can be isolated and measured, giving us remarkable insights into human behavior. From this has come knowledge that enables us to choose a life work in which we can find satisfaction and self-expression, and eliminate those realms where chances of success or contentment are slim. But perhaps the most significant contribution is helping us know ourselves and others better, so needed if there is to be good will and harmony in the world.

Career Suggestions for Various Combinations of Aptitudes

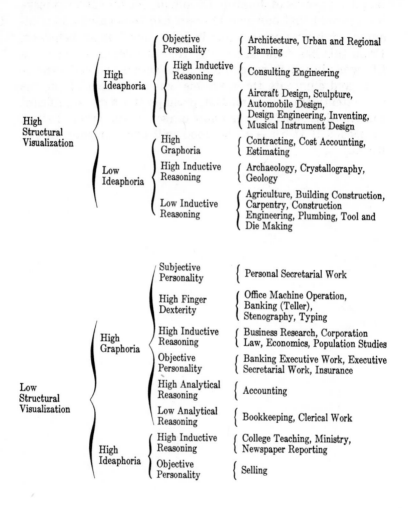

High Structural Visualization

High Ideaphoria
- Objective Personality — Architecture, Urban and Regional Planning
- High Inductive Reasoning — Consulting Engineering
- Aircraft Design, Sculpture, Automobile Design, Design Engineering, Inventing, Musical Instrument Design

Low Ideaphoria
- High Graphoria — Contracting, Cost Accounting, Estimating
- High Inductive Reasoning — Archaeology, Crystallography, Geology
- Low Inductive Reasoning — Agriculture, Building Construction, Carpentry, Construction Engineering, Plumbing, Tool and Die Making

Low Structural Visualization

High Graphoria
- Subjective Personality — Personal Secretarial Work
- High Finger Dexterity — Office Machine Operation, Banking (Teller), Stenography, Typing
- High Inductive Reasoning — Business Research, Corporation Law, Economics, Population Studies
- Objective Personality — Banking Executive Work, Executive Secretarial Work, Insurance
- High Analytical Reasoning — Accounting
- Low Analytical Reasoning — Bookkeeping, Clerical Work

High Ideaphoria
- High Inductive Reasoning — College Teaching, Ministry, Newspaper Reporting
- Objective Personality — Selling

Objective Personality

- **High Inductive Reasoning**
  - **High Structural Visualization**
    - **High Ideaphoria** — Urban and Regional Planning
    - **Low Ideaphoria** — Directing Archaeological Expeditions; Mechanical Repairing on Customer's Premises
  - **Low Structural Visualization**
    - **High Ideaphoria** — Adult Education, Supervision, Advertising, Editorial Work, Publishing, Public Health
    - **Low Ideaphoria** — Police Work
- **Low Inductive Reasoning**
  - **Average Structural Visualization**
    - **Average or High Graphoria** — Manufacturing Executive Work, Engineering Executive Work, Factory Management
    - **High Ideaphoria** — Sales Engineering
  - **Low Structural Visualization**
    - **Average or High Graphoria** — Building Management, Business Management, Food Service Supervision, Executive Work, Hospital Management, Housing Management, Museum Management, Store Management
    - **High Ideaphoria** — Merchandising, Sales Promotion, Store Selling

Subjective Personality

- **High Inductive Reasoning**
  - **High Structural Visualization**
    - **High Ideaphoria** — Medical Research, Scientific Research
    - **Low Ideaphoria** — Diagnostic Medicine, Patent Law, Physiological Chemistry, Paleobotany
  - **Low Structural Visualization** — Book Reviewing, Criminal Law, Historical Writing, Rewrite Work
- **Low Inductive Reasoning**
  - **High Structural Visualization**
    - **High Finger Dexterity** — Hospital Laboratory Work
    - **High Ideaphoria** — Technical Engineering, Amplifier Design, Broadcasting Apparatus Design
  - **Low Structural Visualization**
    - **High Ideaphoria** — Acting, Imaginative Writing

High Inductive Reasoning	Average or High Structural Visualization	High Analytical Reasoning	Computer Programmer
		Subjective Personality	Diagnostic Medicine Patent Law Scientific Research
	Low Structural Visualization	Average or Above Graphoria	Corporation Law
		Subjective Personality	Book Reviewing Criminal Law Historical Writing Law—General Rewrite Work
		Objective Personality	Complaint Work—Department Store Diplomacy International Relations Politics
		High Memory For Design	Art Criticism
		High Analytical Reasoning	Debating Editorial Work Essay Writing
High Ideaphoria	High Structural Visualization	Objective Personality	Architecture
		Subjective Personality	Architectural Sculpture Bookbinding (Design) Dress Design Furniture Design Manufacturing Design Stage Design Window Display
	High Inductive Reasoning	Low Structural Visualization	Classroom Teaching Employee Training Fiction Writing Publicity
	Low Inductive Reasoning	High Memory for Design	Art in Advertising Commercial Design Graphic Arts Interior Decoration
		Objective Personality	Commission Selling Insurance Selling

High Graphoria
- Low Structural Visualization
  - High Analytical Reasoning — Accounting
  - High Number Memory — Library Work
  - Higher Finger Dexterity — Office Machine Operation / Banking (Teller)
  - Average or High Inductive Reasoning — Business Research / Economics / Evaluating Advertising Campaigns / Insurance Adjusting
  - Objective Personality — Banking (General)
- Average or Low Structural Visualization
  - High Tweezer Dexterity — Nursing
- Average or High Structural Visualization
  - Low Ideaphoria — Cost Accounting (Manufacturing) / Estimating
  - High Analytical Reasoning — Actuarial Work

High Tweezer Dexterity
- High Ideaphoria
  - High Structural Visualization
    - Objective Personality — Occupational Therapy, Vocational Training
    - Subjective Personality — Arts and Crafts, Bookbinding, Jewelry Design, Museum Mounting, Sculpture, Wood-Carving
  - Average or Low Structural Visualization
    - Objective Personality — Demonstrating
- Low Ideaphoria
  - High Structural Visualization
    - Subjective Personality — Anatomy, Chemical Analysis, Dentistry, Drafting, Mechanical Crafts, Physiology, Surgery, Watch Repair
  - Average or Low Structural Visualization
    - High Graphoria — Nursing, Nutrition (Laboratory Research)
    - Low Graphoria — Dental Hygiene, Instrument Assembly, Miniature-Instrument Assembly, Mounting Botanical Slides

151

High Tonal Memory
- Objective Personality
  - High Inductive Reasoning { Teaching Music
  - Average Graphoria { Management in the: Theater / Motion Pictures / Radio and Television
  - High Ideaphoria { Selecting and Engaging Musical Talent
  - High Number Memory { Production Control in Television, Radio and Motion Pictures / Scheduling Radio and Television Programs
- Subjective Personality
  - High Graphoria { Musical Performance Piano
  - High Pitch Discrimination { Musical Performance Singing
  - High Inductive Reasoning { Musical Criticism

High Observation
- High Structural Visualization
  - High Tweezer Dexterity { Bacteriology / Histology / Metallography / Microscope Research
  - High Graphoria { Astronomy
- Average or High Structural Visualization
  - Objective Personality { Safety Engineering
- Low Structural Visualization
  - High Inductive Reasoning { Criminology / Descriptive Writing / Newspaper Reporting / Detective work
  - Objective Personality { Inspection Supervision
  - Average or High Graphoria { Insurance Adjusting

High Number Memory
- Objective Personality
  - Low Ideaphoria
    - Average or High Graphoria { Stock Market Trading, Production Following, Expediting
  - High Ideaphoria
    - Average or High Graphoria { Insurance Selling / Store Selling / Securities Selling
- Subjective Personality
  - Average or High Graphoria { Library Work / Stockroom Keeping

152

Human Engineering Laboratories

Human Engineering Laboratory
1349 West Fifth Street
Los Angeles, California 90017   213/481-0911

Human Engineering Laboratory
3004 Sixth Avenue
San Diego, California 92103   714/291-6785

Johnson O'Connor Research Foundation Inc.
Suite 340, 3445 Peachtree Rd., N. E.
Atlanta, Georgia 30326   404/261-8013

Human Engineering Laboratory
161 East Erie Street
Chicago, Illinois 60611   312/787-9141

Human Engineering Laboratory Inc.
347 Beacon Street
Boston, Massachusetts 02116   617/536-0409

Johnson O'Connor Research Foundation Inc.
47 E. Adams Street
Detroit, Michigan 48226   313/963-9185

Johnson O'Connor Research Foundation Inc.
11 East 62nd Street
New York, New York 10021   212/838-0550

Johnson O'Connor Research Foundation Inc.
906 South Cheyenne
Tulsa, Oklahoma 74119   918/583-0620

Human Engineering Laboratory
1518 Walnut Street
Philadelphia, Pennsylvania 19103   215/732-1122

Johnson O'Connor Research Foundation Inc.
650 S. Henderson Street
Fort Worth, Texas 76104   817/335-1867

Johnson O'Connor Research Foundation Inc.
Suite 124, 2055 South Gessner at Ella Lee
Houston, Texas 77063   713/783-3411

Johnson O'Connor Research Foundation Inc.
121 Second Street, N. E.
Washington, D. C. 20002   202/547-3922

Your Natural Gifts

Order Form

Please tear out and mail your order to:
EPM Publications, Inc., Box 442, McLean, Va. 22101

Please send me_____ copies of
YOUR NATURAL GIFTS by Margaret E. Broadley.
1 copy $6.00 (Price includes postage and handling.)
Virginia residents only, add 20¢ sales tax.
Please enclose your check or money order.

Name _____
(Please Print)   First   Initial   Last

Street _____
P.O. Box, or Apt. Number

_____
City   State   Zip